ANDY & ME

Crisis and Transformation on the Lean Journey

Pascal Dennis

PRODUCTIVITY
productivity press

Productivity Press • New York

Most Productivity Press books are available at quantity discounts when purchased in bulk. For more information contact our Customer Service Department (888-319-5852). Address all other inquires to:

Productivity Press
444 Park Avenue South, 7th floor
New York, NY 10016
United States of America
Telephone: 212-686-5900
Fax: 212-686-5411
E-mail: info@productivitypress.com

Text Design and Page composition by Typography Services
Printed and bound by Malloy Lithographing in the United States of America

Lines from "The Scenes of Summer" by Pamela Jane on page 142–143 are used with permission.

Library of Congress Cataloging-in-Publication Data

Dennis, Pascal, 1957–
  Andy & me : crisis and transformation on the lean journey / Pascal Dennis.
    p. cm.
  ISBN 1-56327-298-9 (alk. paper)
  1. Manufacturing processes—Fiction.   2. Production management—Fiction.   3. Just-in-time systems—Fiction.
  4. Production control—Fiction.   I. Title.

PS3604.E5865A53   2005
813'.6—dc22
                                                    2004024417

09 08 07 06 05   5 4

TABLE OF CONTENTS

ACKNOWLEDGMENTS

Thanks to the editorial staff at Productivity Press, and in particular, Michael Sinocchi, Senior Editor, for believing in this project. Thanks to my friend, Allen Sutterfield, who taught me how to write and to Ruth Mills and Janet Rosenstock for their incisive feedback.

Special thanks to my *senseis*—Hiroyuki Watanabe, Takinori Sakaue, Shin Furukawa, John Shook and Erik Hager—with whom it has been my privilege to work. I hope they will overlook the many shortcomings of this book.

I am grateful to Toyota Motor Corporation, which continues to be a beacon to organizations around the world, and whose generosity and openness is helping to make a better world.

This book is dedicated to my three angels—Pamela, Eleanor and Katie.

PREFACE

I initially wrote a bogus Preface that I thought would impress you. When I read it to my better half, Pamela, she rolled her eyes. I decided to pare it down.

Why a novel about the Toyota Production System or lean production?

Well, people seem to like war stories and I make my living teaching the "thinking way." So I wrote one to illustrate it and to show that the West need not become a second- or third-rate industrial power. The "end of Detroit" is not inevitable.

Our banks, hospitals, insurance companies, universities, laboratories and public institutions can also benefit from this profound system of knowledge.

But ultimately, the story simply wanted to be told. The characters took on a life of their own. I just got out of the way.

"We'll Have to Close Some Plants."

I was 37 years old and freshly divorced. I had two little girls whom I adored and a crazy ex-wife who hated me. She was a child of privilege, who was now a society columnist for a major paper. I had once found her beautiful, but now when I looked at her, all I saw was meanness.

My parents had warned me, "Tommy, we don't like this one."

Would I listen? I had always aspired to the mansion on the hill. I didn't know the damned thing was haunted.

Tom Papas is my name. Our family name is Papachristodoulou. I shortened it to fit the back of my football jersey. I grew up on the streets of Astoria, Queens—Greek town. Across the East River we could see Manhattan's glittering skyline, another world.

My parents, Nick and Noula, ran the Humpty Dumpty Bar & Grill, a joint at the corner of 31st Street and Ditmars Blvd. There was a neon sign outside–Humpty taking a header, which seemed an apt metaphor for my life.

If you looked up *Greek restaurateur* in the dictionary you'd see my dad's photo. He had a voice like a trumpet and nose like a rocket ship. "HELLO, NICE LOOKING! BOY

IF I WASN'T MARRIED ..." "HEY CHIEF, YOU HEAR THE ONE ABOUT SPEEDY GONZALEZ?"

Mama was round and cheerful and made Astoria's best spanakopita, a traditional spinach and feta cheese pie that melted in your mouth. She was also a promotional wizard. There was a neon sign in the window: GOOD FOOD. When it lost some letters, Mama had a brainwave.

"Nicky, come stand beneath the sign. I'm going to take your picture."

"Now give me a big smile."

The GOO F photo made Dad "King of Astoria" and the Humpty Dumpty a local landmark. Soon the walls were covered with celebrity photographs. Dad mixing it up with Muhammad Ali. Mama shaking her finger at Marv Albert.

My brother Harry and I helped out as kids. We took customer orders, delivered sandwiches and worked the cash register. It was fun, but our folks wanted a better life for us. Education was sacred.

So I became an engineer, and Harry went into pharmaceuticals. I envy my brother: He gets big bonuses and fat expense accounts—because the industry charges eighty bucks for a little pill. He also has a nice wife, whereas my personal life is a train wreck.

I'm manager of a failing auto plant, which is part of Taylor Motors. The company as a whole is also struggling. Our founder, Alfred Taylor, was an acolyte of Henry Ford and helped invent the auto industry. I love going to our head office in Motown and seeing our logo on building after building. I love the Product Design Center and the test track. I love the Automotive Hall of Fame and the old Taylor farm, now turned into a museum.

The 20th century was our century, we used to say. Would we say the same thing about the 21st century?

We had gone through bad times before, especially in the 1930s and the 1980s when it looked like we might go under. But we always bounced back. There was just too much car-making know-how.

But now we keep losing market share—mainly in the car market, and mainly to the Japanese. Trucks are our bread and butter; we're number two behind Ford. Even here, Toyota, Honda and Nissan are making inroads. Each is aggressively expanding truck production and taking direct aim at us.

Their quality has always been better. Their unit costs are a thousand bucks lower. How the hell do they produce better quality at lower cost?

Our plant, New Jersey Motor Manufacturing, is just outside of Union City. We make the Desperado, a muscle car with a 3.8 liter V8 engine and great styling. The public loves it. In fact, they want us to make 940 units a day. Last year, we missed delivery on over 4,000 units—about 20 every day. Because we're the only Taylor plant making the Desperado, each was a lost sale. Things have been better this year, but only because I've been running as much overtime as I can wrangle out of the union. This has blown my labor budget. Last year, I got hammered on delivery; this year, it will be cost.

Why do we lose production? Machine breakdowns, poor quality, part shortages, people not showing up for work; you name it.

Machine availability is poor, especially in our Welding Department. Our maintenance people run from breakdown to breakdown barking into their radios. Some freak out. "I can't handle this anymore," a young maintenance engineer told me at his exit interview. He said he was going into real estate.

Preventative maintenance seems an impossible dream. Last week a pipe burst and flooded our Assembly shop. We lost a whole shift. Guess who had to work on Saturday?

We have quality problems in all our major departments—Stamping, Body, Paint and Assembly. There is a big "repair hospital" at the end of our final line—and it's always full. Every morning at 8:00 A.M., we have a Customer Audit where we look at Desperados that have come back with defects. We keep getting the same electrical problems, water leaks, wrong and missing parts, and the like. Yet, we have good people who work long hours. So why can't we do what we're trying to do?

Maybe it's my fault. Used to be I could deliver results through sheer willpower. I was the Boy Wonder, the wizard who had saved the Desperado plant. I drove my team hard, and they never failed me. But I can't seem to generate the same intensity. I feel lousy much of the time. What is wrong with me?

It's a bone-chilling January morning. We've just finished our 6:30 A.M. start-up meeting. I'm walking back through the Welding shop, which is dark as a cave. Spark showers pierce the gloom, the noise is deafening and I can smell hot metal. Forklift trucks lumber past me carrying racks full of doors, hoods and fenders. Dirt and grease is everywhere.

I'm wearing safety glasses, ear plugs and my ratty old Desperado jacket. I can't bring myself to throw it out. We all got one when the Desperado won the gold medal for quality. It seems a lifetime ago.

I walk out a side door and into the cold, gray light. Snow scrunches under my feet as I walk past the scrap yard. It's full of twisted car bodies–yesterday's casualties. We'll sell them off as scrap metal.

When I get to the front office, I see Bill Barrett's Desperado Mach III out front. As I walk past reception, I give Anne, my intrepid assistant, the Vulcan salute. "Where is the old goat?"

"He's in your office," she says, "with his feet on your desk."

Bill Barrett is my boss, a big Liverpudlian with silver hair, a scarlet nose and a love of early rock and roll. He is the director of manufacturing in charge of four plants on the East Coast, including our own.

Bill grew up with the Beatles and claims he once punched out Ringo Starr. I like his accent. He is a good man who has helped me through some rough times.

"How are you, Tommy?"

"Not good, Bill. Same old stuff. Teal is busting my chops, the legal bills are killing me and we can't make enough good cars. How about you?"

"I'm maintaining, Tommy. Marjorie's been acting up lately."

It was our common bond. We both had nasty ex-wives.

"What's up, Bill?" I ask him.

He gets up and closes the door. "Wall Street is saying we won't meet our cost reduction targets. Word on the street is we need to merge with Ford or GM, but they don't want us. The stock's getting hammered. Our bonds are being downgraded. We'll have to close some plants. "

I sit down.

"Union City is on the hit list, Tommy."

I try to take it in. New Jersey Motor Manufacturing has sustained working people for 50 years. People like my parents. Almost 3,000 souls and their families depend on me. And I'm letting let them down.

"How much time do we have, Bill?"

"A year, maybe less."

We walk out to the Assembly shop floor, which is bright with activity. Clarence, our final line supervisor, waves and grins. "Good to see you, Mr. Barrett. Hey Tom, got your mojo working yet?"

Clarence and I go way back. And everyone knows about my marital problems. "My mojo's dead, Clarence."

Laughter. "No, Tommy. My cousin's gonna bring you something from Jamaica."

"How about his sister?" More laughter.

"You don't want her!"

"I'll take her!" says Bill.

We're all laughing now. I feel better. "How's our quality today, Clarence?"

"Not good, Tommy. We've already had fifteen chips and scratches and seven water leaks. I don't know what they're doing on night shift."

"I don't either, Clarence. Please give Anne the VIN numbers. We'll take it up at our end-of-shift meeting."

We walk through final line watching the assembly process. Same old pock-marked floors and dented columns.

Same old tin ceiling way up, way up in the gloom. Forklift trucks rumble by; there are parts everywhere.

The "hospital" is full of beautiful Desperados.

What am I going to do?

Looking for Mr. Saito

That's how I got to looking for Andy Saito. I'd heard he was a manufacturing genius, the heavyweight who had led Toyota's international expansion. He had launched plants all over the world, including three in America's heartland.

Then he disappeared.

A pal of mine, Dean Formica, had worked for Saito at Toyota's Kentucky plant. Dino is a boy from the old neighborhood with a droll view of the world. We went for a beer last month when he was in town for Christmas. He had just been promoted to General Manager at the Toyota Kentucky Paint shop and was pretty happy about it.

"Congratulations, amico," I told him, clinking glasses.

"Thanks," he said. "Cente anni–may we live a hundred years."

Toyota Kentucky is a huge plant–about seven million square feet, with 6,000 people producing 600,000 Camrys and Siennas a year. Despite the chaos of continual expansion, they keep winning quality and productivity awards.

Toyota makes more cars outside Japan than in it. They have staked their future on North America, and Kentucky is the cornerstone. I remembered that Dino had talked about the Toyota Production System, or TPS, with reverence. He had sounded like Caine in the old *Kung Fu* TV series. And I had had some fun with this. "Another beer, grasshopper?"

"You can laugh, Tommy, but it's the real deal. The right way to manage."

He also had told me some stories about Saito, whom he had called his "sensei." I'd never heard Dino speak about anyone like that.

Apparently, Saito had flamed out. There were rumors of depression, alcoholism. Dean had said he didn't know any more, and he wouldn't speculate. But rumor had it that Saito was living somewhere in New Jersey.

"You ought to call him, man. He can help you turn that rat-hole around." Dino knew all about our problems. "By the way, he *loves* aikido."

I had studied aikido in my teens. Harry and I used to take the subway to the dojo on West 18th Street. Our sensei was Mr. Chiba, a jovial bear who threw us around like rag dolls. Chiba had once appeared on *The Mike Douglas Show* and had tossed Mike into the audience. Chiba-sensei is still teaching and has been trying to get on *Survivor*.

So after Bill Barrett broke the terrible news that our plant might go under, I decided to find Saito. What did we have to lose?

I had been through several Toyota plants, both in North America and in Japan. I had been to workshops on the Toyota Production System or lean production. But I didn't really understand it. Only that Toyota was kicking our butts, and doing it on our own turf.

There was no Andy Saito in the phone book. So I gave Anne the task of finding all the aikido clubs and Japanese cultural centers in the state. She is a great lady with two grown sons and a new grandchild. She keeps trying to set me up on blind dates, but I usually beg off. "I'm too screwed up," I tell her.

So here I am on Saturday morning driving the interstate, working through the list Anne has given me. It's a beautiful day, but I feel lousy. My ex-wife wouldn't let me talk to my girls this morning. I had brought them home 10 minutes late. She lives in a condo on the Upper East Side. Every Wednesday I leave the plant early and struggle through the Lincoln tunnel and central Manhattan traffic to spend a few hours with my children. And I brought them home late.

"Why do I *always* have to use the *two-by-four* on you?" she said.

It's the same routine each place I visit. "Would you know a man named Takinori Saito, also known as Andy? Former Toyota executive? Loves aikido?" I work my way through the local Jersey towns: Fairview, North Bergen, Secaucus. Nothing.

I luck out at the Japanese Cultural Center in Jersey City. "Yes, we know Saito-san. Who are you?" I give them my business card and explain my intent. I tell them I'm Mr. Chiba's student.

Mr. Nakamura, the director, invites me into his office. He is an elegant old dude with a humorous expression. "Very pleased to meet you. Chiba-sensei is a great friend of our center. Mr. Saito used to practice aikido here. But now he mainly comes to meditation class."

"Is he alright?"

"Could be better."

"Maybe I should leave the man alone."

"No. It may be good for Mr. Saito to work again. I will call him on your behalf."

Nakamura spends 10 minutes on the phone speaking Japanese while I admire the calligraphy on the wall. Reminds me of the stuff we had in the old dojo. Finally, he turns to me. "Mr. Saito will see you tomorrow at two o'clock, after meditation class."

Well, well, well, I thought. Maybe our luck is changing.

Finding a Sensei

The next day I returned to the Japanese Cultural Center at 1:30. It was a beautiful winter day, sunlight pouring down. I hadn't expected to spend my whole weekend looking for this guy, but I would do anything at this point to save the plant. I walked past the Japanese rock garden, through the glass doors and into the dojo. I bowed, took off my shoes and sat on the bench against the back wall. The floor was covered with well-worn tatami mats. On the wall there were photos of Mr. Kano and Mr. Ueshiba, the great senseis who had founded judo and aikido, respectively. I had bowed to both photos many times.

It was pleasingly dim in the dojo. There were about 20 people in the class. Which one was Andy? I shut my eyes and began to breathe deeply like Mr. Chiba taught me. Images began to drift by . . . my kids, parents, people at the plant. My neck and shoulders were tight. I had a headache.

I inhaled and exhaled, concentrating on my "one-point," the spot two inches below my navel, from which my being apparently emanates. Where did I learn this stuff? My mind drifted to my last conversation with my ex-wife.

"You brought the children home late again!"

"Relax, Teal, it was ten minutes."

"No! I won't relax. Sophie is only six. She is always tired after spending time with you."

"I only get three hours with them, Teal. You know what traffic is like. We had dinner in Astoria then went for ice cream. I don't think ten minutes is a big deal. Relax."

"No, no, no! I won't relax. *You're* the problem, Tom. You owe me ten minutes. You are not living up to our agreement. Do you think I *enjoy* waiting for you? What are you going to do to *ensure* this doesn't happen again? You'd better have an answer if you want to see the children next Wednesday."

I wanted to say something nasty. Somehow I held my tongue.

Images continued to drift by. I saw little Sophie running toward me, "Daddy, Daddy, Daddy" and leaping into my arms. Helen, my oldest, looked up at me with her large eyes and delicate neck, "I want to see more of you, Daddy. But Mommy says it isn't going to work out."

Then I was in the Paint shop, looking at cars on the inspection deck. Bright lights, shiny metal, hum of the conveyors. We had been having a terrible time with spits and mars. Where was the dirt coming from?

Then I was back in the dojo inhaling and exhaling. This too shall pass.

Someone cleared his throat. "Papa-san?"

I opened my eyes; the dojo was empty. A Japanese man stood before me in a well-worn judo gi and black belt. Hawk eyes, moustache, hair streaked with silver and longer than you'd expect in an executive. He looked about 60 and was grinning expectantly, as a child might. I liked him.

"Papa-san?"

"That would be me. Please call me Tom."

"Takinori Saito. Please call me Andy. Who taught you how to meditate?"

"Chiba-sensei of New York Aikikai."

"Ah! You are an aikidoka. Very good! How can I help you?"

I told him everything.

"Dean-san is a friend of yours?"

"One of my best. We grew up together. He speaks very highly of you."

"Dean-san is a hard worker. Good thinking way. We built Kentucky Paint shop together."

"Can you help us?"

He sighed. "Taylor Motor is a great company. I have learned much from Alfred Taylor. Mr. Nakamura would like me to work again. But I don't know if I have the strength, the motivation. If one cannot do a good job, must not start work."

"Maybe I can help you. My brother knows the best doctors in the state. My company would be happy to . . ."

He shook his head. "No need. Thank you."

"Mr. Saito, we are going to lose our plant. People I care about will lose their jobs. All I know about you is what Dean told me. But I think you can help us. I'm a hard worker and I listen."

Saito looked at me. "The Toyota way is a severe way. Not one or two months. Not one or two years, but a whole lifetime. Please understand. If you are not serious, do not start."

"Mr. Saito, I'll do whatever is necessary to save our plant."

He looked at me again. "Do you like hamburgers?"

"Yes, I do."

"How about French fries with cheese?"

"You mean New York fries. My Dad practically invented them."

"Ah, very good," he laughed. "How about bourbon?"

I nod. An unusual lunch, but what the hell.

"Okay. I will change now and meet you across the street in twenty minutes."

He turned and walked away, leaving me with Kano and Ueshiba. I wasn't sure what had just happened. But I felt I knew this man. And I felt he could help us.

Sincere Mind

We ordered cheeseburgers, New York fries and bourbon on the rocks. I told Andy everything. He listened quietly, occasionally closing his eyes. When I finished speaking, he looked out the window. "You have many problems, Tom-san."

Andy and I agreed that we would talk some more. I knew enough about the Japanese not to push it. We had to get to know one another. It was all a matter of trust and respect.

Andy seemed ambivalent, despite his obvious interest in what was happening at the plant. Was he uncomfortable working with a Toyota competitor? Was there some family problem, some illness? I sure hoped he wasn't an alcoholic—and though I at first thought it was odd that Andy drank bourbon with cheeseburgers, I remembered he had drunk only one.

Over the next few weeks we had lunch several times. I even took in a meditation class at the Japanese Cultural Center. Andy said that he had spoken to Japan and that they had given him the go-ahead. We talked about how we might structure our working relationship. I persuaded him to visit the plant.

It was a gray January morning, but at least the cold spell had broken. Andy arrived at 7:30 A.M. sharp with his safety boots and glasses. I was coming back from Paint shop and found him in reception kibitzing with Anne. "I like him," she whispered.

When we hit the shop floor Andy seemed to grow taller, broader. His pace quickened, and I had a hard time keeping up. Andy had asked that we "walk the process" from steel coil receipt in Stamping to the loading of Desperados in the rail yard. The plant was a mess, as usual. Andy frequently stopped to pick up bolts, paper and other garbage.

"You don't have to do that, Saito-san."

He gave me a puzzled look. "Tripping hazard, Tom-san." As we walked, he pointed out several more hazards and suggested "countermeasures" for each one.

"What is your pinch point standard?" he asked.

"Ah, we don't have one."

Andy checked emergency stop buttons, safety mats and fire extinguishers. Why was he so interested in safety? He certainly liked talking to workers. In the Assembly shop, he stopped to talk to a young guy, who I knew had just started with us. I suppose Andy chose him because he looked new to the job and therefore might have a fresh opinion. The guy was on strut install, one of our toughest processes.[1]

"My name is Andy Saito. May I ask you about your job?"

The guy didn't know how to react. "I guess so."

"How is ergonomics on this job?"

---

1. By 'process' I mean a repeated series of steps with a specific cycle time. Andy also used the terms 'job' and 'operation.' We had about 300 processes in our plant.

"Well, these struts are really heavy," said the guy. "My shoulders ache at the end of the day."

"Any other problems?" Andy asked.

The guy looked anxious, thinking he might be in trouble.

"It's okay," I told him. "We're just trying to understand how to make the work easier."

"Ah, wire harnesses come wrapped in cellophane, which is a pain to remove. And the jig doesn't always release. I fall behind a lot."

Andy looked over at me. "Machine, method and material problems, Tom-san."

Then he continued his discussion with the guy. "Do you rotate to other jobs?"

"No."

"What do you do if there is a quality problem?"

"I tell my team leader."

"When?"

"When I see him."

"What if you don't see him?" The guy shrugged.

Andy frowned at several other jobs in Assembly, especially the steering column install process.

Andy watched a young kid bend into the car and bolt the steering column to the floor. It was a lousy job to which low seniority workers were assigned. The nut-runner was heavy and vibrated like crazy.

"Ergonomics, Tom-san! How can one work in such a posture? How can one make quality?"

He spent a good deal of time just watching. In the Body shop we stood in the same spot for 40 minutes watching the wheelhouse team assemble the structures into which the wheels would fit. Bang-shush-rumble-crash, bang-shush-rumble-crash—the rhythm of metal on metal, compressed air lines and conveyors.

Andy discretely timed each process and then made a bar chart of cycle time versus what he called *takt* time. Each bar was broken up into two main segments and annotated in Japanese. I copied it out later in English to make sure I understood what he had taught me.

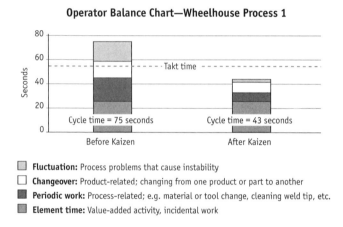

Operator Balance Chart—Wheelhouse Process 1

☐ **Fluctuation:** Process problems that cause instability
☐ **Changeover:** Product-related; changing from one product or part to another
■ **Periodic work:** Process-related; e.g. material or tool change, cleaning weld tip, etc.
■ **Element time:** Value-added activity, incidental work

"Takt line shows customer demand," Andy said. "One unit every 58 seconds. The operator balance chart shows value and waste. You have much waste in each operation, Tom-san."

Then he showed me a series of balance charts for the entire wheelhouse team—current, improved and "rebalanced." How had he seen so much?

Balance Chart—Wheelhouse Team

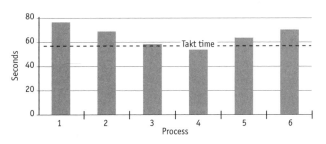

Balance Chart—with Kaizen

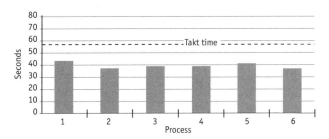

Wheelhouse Team—After Rebalancing

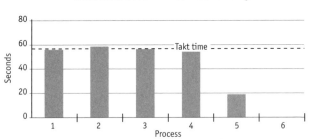

"You have six workers in wheelhouse, Tom-san. But you need only five. Later on, with kaizen you can reduce the number to four."

My mind was doing the cha-cha. "What do you mean by kaizen, Mr. Saito?"

"Small continuous improvement. Like a samurai honing his blade."

He made a cutting gesture with his hand, as Chiba-sensei used to in our aikido dojo. "Every day our eyes become sharper! Every day our team becomes stronger!"

"But you've just eliminated two people from the wheel-house team."

"We must never eliminate team members," said Andy. "Instead, we eliminate waste and reassign people to more valuable work."

He slammed the table where we sat, startling me. "We must have respect for humanity. Why should a team member waste his energy, his time, his mind?"

It had never occurred to me. Work was lousy. That's just the way it was.

"The key to productivity," Andy continued, "is not to make more, but to use less effort!"

He had unsettled me. I had been taught to think in units per hour, the more the better. You can only build to customer demand if you have reliable machines and processes. We didn't, so every day we just made as many as we could. Nobody was ever reprimanded for making too much.

"Sensei, what's wrong with making more than the customer wants?"

Andy looked at me like I was from outer space. I made a mental note to call Dean Formica for help. I didn't want to seem like a total idiot.

Then Andy smiled. "Ah, yes. I'm sorry Tom-san. You have not had Toyota training."

Then patiently and at length, Andy explained that overproduction was the worst of the Seven Wastes because it caused every other kind of waste. At Taylor Motors we had been taught to think in terms of units per hour, which fostered our "move the metal" mentality. But at Toyota the focus was on the process. Could it be completed safely— and with quality, within takt time? Hence, the importance of kaizen and team member involvement.

I was embarrassed at how little I knew. I began to grasp the chasm between Toyota and us. I began to grasp why Toyota plants didn't need big repair hospitals. And why our plant was full of sick Desperados.

I felt momentarily depressed. How could we change decades-old thinking?

When we parted Andy gave me a list of books to read. I had found my sensei, if he would accept me as a deshi.

———————

The next day I was on the phone to Bill Barrett. "Saito is the real deal, Bill. But I don't know if he'll work with us. He seems ambivalent. And he got really annoyed by what he saw on our shop floor."

"Let's have a teleconference with Rachel," Bill said.

Rachel Armstrong is senior vice-president of North American operations and Bill's boss. We call her the "Iron

Lady." She won't tolerate bullshit, and her temper is legendary. But she treats people fairly and with respect.

Rachel worked with W. Edwards Deming, the American quality guru, when he was very old. Deming is credited with igniting the "Japanese miracle." Rachel had reintroduced Deming's thinking when she became Senior VP two years ago: Plan-do-check-adjust; control defects at the source; understand variation; and so on. We'd heard it all before in the 1980s but it didn't really take. The move-the-metal attitude was too strongly ingrained.

Rachel had also told us that Toyota would be our benchmark. "They've extended and deepened Deming's teaching. They've lapped us and we don't even know it."

This caused a lot of grumbling.

"Who won the war anyhow?" asked a veteran plant manager.

"Not you," I thought.

But we were in good company. General Motors, Ford and Chrysler had already launched their own versions of the Toyota Production System. Now we were all "Toyota guys"—whatever that meant.

Rachel faces many obstacles, not the least of which is J. Edwin Morgan a.k.a. the Prince of Darkness. Morgan is our CFO and has a stranglehold on the company. The standing joke is senior executives can't go to the john without Morgan's approval.

Morgan believes in managing by the numbers—the accounting numbers. Every week he and his Ivy League robots scrutinize our labor and machine "efficiencies." Each department in each plant has to meet "standard." We do contortions to make the numbers look right.

We plant managers like and respect Rachel but are ambivalent about the Toyota stuff. "All well and good in theory," we say. "But we still have to build cars under ridiculous constraints."

For example, each year Morgan strips out more of our "nonessential" resources. I've lost half of my team leaders and half of my HR department. There is no money for machinery, even though our stamping and welding equipment is 20 years old. And our collective agreement has 84 job classifications. That means that I can't assign people to do work that needs doing.

How would Toyota handle that?

Bill's assistant, Jennifer, called me back an hour later. "Bill and Rachel are on line three."

Rachel got excited when I told her about Andy. "Holy cow! I'd be thrilled to have Mr. Saito come on board as a consultant. He's just what we need."

"I don't know if he'll work with us, Rachel," I said.

"I'll call him," she said. "We'll have to show progress quickly—meaning this year. Please think about how we might extend the learning beyond Union City. Now if you gentlemen will excuse me, I have a meeting with that pinhead Morgan."

A couple of days later I was in the Stamping shop watching a die changeover when my cell phone rang. It was Andy.

"Ah, Papa-san, konnichiwa!"

"Konnichiwa, Mr. Saito."

"Maybe I can help New Jersey Motor Manufacturing." Hey now!

"But you must agree to some conditions. You must make safety priority number one. Ergonomics is bad. You must develop an ergonomic strategy. Also, there are too many pinch points and blind corners.

"Next, you must clean and paint factory. Work areas are in bad condition. Garbage is everywhere! I will make a list. You fix. One last thing, when I give assignments, you must do. Discuss yes. Argue no. Okay?"

I agreed.

The next day Andy and Bill came into the plant and we spent a couple of hours confirming the details. Andy would spend several days a week with us. He'd give assignments and we'd learn by doing. Rachel had found us respectable consulting dollars and money for cleaning, painting and safety upgrades. But money didn't seem to interest Andy.

Bill, Andy and I agreed on the following targets to be achieved by year end:

- 20% improvement in our main safety, quality, delivery and cost indicators.
- 25% reduction in ergonomic burden (whatever that is).

"If we meet these targets, we should be okay," said Bill. It was late January. We had eleven months.

We clinched the deal over bourbon at the Iron Horse, a joint a few blocks from the plant. Andy ordered Makers Mark bourbon. He said he learned to drink it in Kentucky. Bill and I followed suit. I poured two fingers of water into mine. Andy and Bill took theirs straight.

We clinked glasses. "Here's to New Jersey Motor Man-ufacturing," I said. "Long may she run."

"And to Andy Saito," said Bill, turning on the blarney. "Welcome to the team. We're proud to have you."

Andy bowed. "It is my pleasure."

I took a sip of bourbon. "I have a question, sensei. Why is safety so important?"

Again, Andy just looked at me. "Sincere mind, Tom-san. Through safety we express sincere mind."

"I don't understand."

"Tom-san, to make quality car we need four M's: man and woman, method, machine and material. Most important is the team member. If we do not take care of team members, we cannot make a good car."

Again, the thought had never occurred to me. Was I stupid?

"Mr. Saito," said Bill, reading my mind, "We have a great deal to learn."

Henry Ford's Vision

I ended up in the business because as a kid I was fascinated with Henry Ford. It all started with a grade school project. I read Henry's autobiography, *Today and Tomorrow*, and that was it. Here is a man who doubled wages, cut the price of a car in half and built over two million units a year.

A century ago making automobiles was a craft business. You'd give your specs to a local job shop, usually run by an entrepreneur who did a range of work. What he couldn't do himself, he'd farm out. Several months later you'd get your car. You'd road test it with the mechanic, who'd modify it to your liking. It was handmade and one of a kind. Ferrari and Lamborghini still make cars in much the same way.

As a customer it must have been great to deal with the manufacturer directly, to get personal attention like that. There were more than 500 car manufacturers back then. Those old dudes knew a lot about design, machining and fitting. There was no such thing as a spark plug or a carburettor. Camshafts, push rods, bearings, piston rings and gears had to be made from scratch. Each part wasn't just one problem—it was a series of problems. This was costly—

only the rich could afford a car. Quality was dicey and repair difficult.

Meanwhile, a young mechanic and entrepreneur named Henry Ford was trying to design a car that was easy to manufacture and repair. He had a vision: a simple, cheap and durable car for the common people. After several bankruptcies he finally succeeded in 1908 with the Model T. Over the next decade Ford invented a system that could turn out quality cars at lower and lower prices.

Henry had a knack for finding the right people. As he roamed the shop floor, men like investor Alexander Malcolmson, finance expert James Cousins and management guru Alfred Taylor tended the business. Taylor in particular provided the structure and focus that harnessed Henry's creative power.

We call it mass production and are blasé about it. But it was an astonishing feat. Every year, cars got cheaper *and* better. Between 1908 and the early 1920s, when annual production hit two million units, Ford had cut the real cost to the customer by two-thirds. The efficiencies realized thereby allowed him to double the wage of his workers, which outraged his fellow industrialists.

Henry's manufacturing innovations are legendary:

- Standard gauging, faithfully used.
- Design for ease of assembly and part interchangeability.
- Fewer moving parts in engines and sub-systems.
- The assembly line.

He did it through tinkering. I love the old photographs of Henry in the shop, sleeves rolled up, monkeeing around. Dean Formica told me the Japanese revere Ford. Apparently, Eiji Toyoda came to Detroit and was graciously received. He never forgot his debt, saying, "I learned everything from Ford."

Henry Ford brought freedom and style to working people, and he paid them a decent wage. Charlie Chaplin made fun of the Ford system in *Modern Times*—and he was right. Henry's system lost its soul as the company grew. People became proverbial cogs in a vast machine whose motto seemed to be *Check your mind at the door*.

But here's the rub. Would we have had the money and leisure to enjoy Charlie's films without mass production? I doubt it. The truth is we'd be miserable without it. So how do we *humanize* it?

Taylor and Ford parted company in 1924. Alfred's vision—"a car for every purse"—contradicted Henry's— "any colour as long as it's black." Alfred's vision would prevail in the long run. Taylor Motors was founded the following year.

Building one good car a day is an achievement. Building a thousand is a miracle. A car is made up of ten thousand parts or more. These have to come together at the right time, in the right order, at the right cost and with the required quality.

The number of failure modes is overwhelming. Consider a water leak at the passenger window. Contributing causes could include the glass, molding, door fit, weld quality and sealer application. Each sits on a thicket of possible subcauses. A given leak can be any combination or permutation. Pretty soon you have a fault tree that looks like a mangrove. And water leaks are only one of hundreds of critical quality elements. My head hurts just thinking about it.

Our plant is a river with many tributaries. We try to balance flow within and between departments so that 58 cars an hour come off our Final line. A breakdown anywhere along the line can stop the flow. To protect ourselves, we put in buffers. There are piles of parts at each workstation; our parts warehouse is a labyrinth.

Our plant is also a chessboard. Our opponent is entropy—decay, chaos, Death, if you will. Entropy always wins in the end. This old plant will be gone some day, as will all of us who work here. But if you're good, you can play him to a standstill. You can even push him back for a while.

To build a great car you also need heart. Our plant is an opera set where soaring passions are played out each day. The passion you need to make beautiful things, to unravel a thousand Gordion knots, to overcome ego, arrogance and pettiness and become a team.

River, chessboard, opera set—that's how I saw our plant. How did Andy see it?

My apprenticeship began the next day. I began to see what Andy saw.

Walking the Plant

I arranged for a detailed plant walkthrough with Andy. I wanted him to see things up-close and to introduce him to each shop manager. It was another awful February morning. I scraped ice off my windshield as the car rumbled to life.

Driving into the plant parking lot, I noticed that the gate was missing. Then I saw Travon, one of our facility maintenance men. He was wearing his yellow traffic vest and carrying a long piece of two-by-four.

"Not again," I said.

"Afraid so, Tom. Some idiot drove through the gate."

"How often does this happen, Travon?"

"I'd say it happens once a week," he said. "Maintaining this gate is a full-time job."

The sky was as bleak as our prospects. "Travon, if we can't follow the simplest rules, how are we going to turn the plant around?"

"I don't know, boss."

To build a Desperado you have to stamp it, weld it, paint it and stuff it. Rail cars bring coils of sheet metal to the

Stamping or Press shop. Blanking machines cut it into rectangular blanks, which are fed into our presses. These bring matching upper and lower dies together to create doors, hoods, floor panels and other parts.

Dies can weigh 30,000 pounds. Billy Taylor, one of our veterans, has only half a left hand. Twenty years ago he got it caught between a die and the wall. "My hand just vaporized," he says.

Our five stamping lines do about 120 strokes a minute and make the ground shake. Stamped parts are sent to our cavernous Stamping warehouse.

Antonio Villareal is the Stamping shop manager, a hip and creative Mexican who came to us from Mazda. Antonio wears his hair in a ponytail. He designs theater sets in his spare time and is irresistible to women.

Antonio is a fine manager and a team player. He's frustrated though. "So many breakdowns, Tom, it drives me crazy." The maintenance boys bust his chops over his ponytail (and his effect on the ladies). "Make a plan and go for it," I told him. "Leave them to me."

Antonio was thrilled to meet Andy. "Konnichiwa, Mr. Saito. It's an honor."

Andy returned his bow. "We have much work to do." He carried a small black notebook, much like a cop's.

The key to effective stamping is maintenance and cleanliness. Poor die maintenance and a dirty shop mean surface defects and parts that don't fit. Quick changeover is also important; it allows you to switch from doors to fenders with a minimal production loss. Our die changes take an hour. Watching one, Andy almost fell asleep. Antonio was embarrassed. "Toyota's take ten minutes," he whispered.

Andy summarized his observations for Antonio and me in the Stamping team room. Again, I marveled at how much he had seen. Antonio thanked Andy and said he would take action and report back within a week.

Andy and I then walked over to the Welding or Body shop where parts are welded into body-sides, undercarriages, front and rear structures. We also add a black sealer to keep water out of critical areas. The Body shop is long, low and dark as a cave. Dirt covers the big round lights suspended from the ceiling. It's hot in summer and noisy year-round: transformers, compressed air lines, metal clattering on metal. Newer plants have air conditioning and quiet machines. I wish I had some money to spend.

About half our welding is done manually, with big C- and X-shaped spot welding guns. The rest is done by robots. My favorite zone is the underbody area where parallel robot lines do a mechanical ballet.

The car body starts as a jigsaw puzzle and comes together at Body buck. Then the roof, fenders, doors, trunk, hood and gas tank are installed.

A good weld requires current, connection and cooling water. You have to hit the right spot solidly, at the right angle and with the right amperage. Water lines suck out the blistering heat. Occasionally, they burst and we get puddles. The most common weld defects are missing, off-location and substandard welds.

Welding is machine-intensive. Robots, multi-welders, conveyors, transfers ... all have to be maintained. Without robust machines you're dead. We're vulnerable because our machines are old.

John Sylvain, the Body shop manager, is my nemesis. He's a burly New Englander with an impeccable pedigree: an alumnus of the MIT Sloan School of Management and a Harvard MBA. He's also married to Peggy Taylor, Alfred's great-granddaughter.

Sylvain has already been manager of Stamping, Paint and Assembly. They are "rounding out" his experience, grooming him for bigger things. Sylvain has energy, ambition and a good manufacturing mind. Rumor has it he wants my job. But he's never left a footprint anywhere he's been. No improvement, no systems, no successor.

Sylvain doesn't believe hourly team members should be involved in production decisions. He runs his shop from the Body control room through banks of computers. Problems are handled by engineers. Workers do as they are told.

Sylvain is enamoured with his Virtual Manufacturer software, which tells him what's happening machine by machine. If it's so good why can't he improve delivery, quality or cost? He has been after me to invest even more in Virtual Manufacturer and to hire more engineers.

Nor does Sylvain believe in what he calls "foreign" manufacturing practices. He wasn't impressed when I told him about Andy.

"Tom, we're Taylor Motors. Toyota learned everything from us," he told me.

"Well, now they're teaching us, John."

"But Japanese workers aren't like ours," he continued. "They do as they're told. You could never trust our people with a line-stop, for example. The union would shut us down in no time."

So John runs the Body shop with an iron fist. He keeps a length of two-by-four, which he calls the "board of education." When things are going badly, he'll call a team meeting. He walks around waving that thing like Robert DeNiro in *The Untouchables*. Then he smashes it on the table. "Do I have everyone's full attention?"

When I confronted him about it, he said, "Come on, Tom. Sometimes you've got to be a bit *crispy*."

"Please don't do that again," I told him.

Sylvain smiled when I introduced Andy to him. "I've heard a lot about you."

Sylvain showed us the control room where his engineers ran the department through Virtual Manufacturer.

"Do they also go see the shop floor?" Andy asked.

"If they have too," said Sylvain.

Sylvain is a favorite of our CFO, the nefarious J. Edwin Morgan, a.k.a. the Prince of Darkness. As I said, Morgan believes in managing "by the numbers." Every week his goons scrutinize our "efficiencies." Sylvain's numbers always look the best, even though his shop runs no better—and often worse—than the others.

Morgan is an accounting genius. Too bad he's not a manufacturing genius. The closer our "efficiencies" get to 100 percent, the worse we seem to do. Some months we're at 110 percent—even though we're losing money. What kind of accounting system is that?

I had shown Andy our accounting reports before our walkthrough. He shook his head. "These reports have no meaning. What about the cost of over-production or bad quality? The focus on direct labor is misleading. What about indirect labor, maintenance and repair?"

"It's voodoo," I said.

"Yes, Tom-san. Accounting systems must be simple. What is the total cost each hour? Include direct and indirect labor, machine cost, space cost and so on. What is output each hour? What is quality and lead time? Basic, basic"

"I like that approach, sensei. But I'm concerned. If our numbers look bad, Jed Morgan may try to shut us down. Or he might try to fire me and make Sylvain plant manager."

"I will speak with Bill-san and Rachel-san," said Andy.

All this was in the back of my mind as Sylvain demonstrated the wonders of Virtual Manufacturer. Andy watched politely. When it was over, he praised Sylvain for the "good software" and summarized his observations. As in Stamping, he had identified our weak spots.

Sylvain waited quietly for Andy to finish. "Thanks for your insight, Mr. Saito. Can we chat some more later this week? I have to pick up my wife."

Andy nodded and bowed politely to Sylvain. "Thanks, John," I said. "Could you please respond to each of Mr. Saito's points by the end of the week?"

Sylvain smiled. "Certainly, Tom."

Continuing the Tour

I've always loved the Paint shop. Imagine bright lights on clean painted metal, elegant robots and vast overhead spaces filled with white ventilation ducts. All air entering the paint shop is filtered, and then filtered again. Dirt means defects. You have to wear a Tyvek suit and a hairnet to get in. To get to our spray booths you have to go through a dust blow-off zone.

Freddie Henderson, our Paint shop manager, is a shy Kentuckian and a gentleman in the truest sense. He is a devout Christian who is devoted to his wife and two daughters. Their pictures cover his office—three beautiful blondes.

Freddie has one unsettling habit—chewing tobacco. There is always a wad in his left cheek, and he often punctuates sentences by leaning over the garbage can and letting fly. "I don't know why we're getting all these craters, Tom." Hork, splat.

"I can't imagine," I say.

The car body comes through the tunnel from Body shop, is dipped in a phosphate tank and sent through a series of rinses. Then it goes into the E-coat tank where it gets an electro-galvanized coating. Next is the metal repair booth where we fix metal defects. These include dents, "updings," weld spatter, splits and poor fit. Some units are so bad that we have to pull them off the line.

Metal repair was swamped when we got there. There were cars all over the place. "Freddie, is this a normal day?" I asked.

He nodded. "Sylvain ships a lot of garbage, Tom. He knows how to play the game. You keep shipping cars to absorb the overhead. Let them pay for it downstream."

We walked over to the sealer line where a sticky white sealer is applied to seams. I stopped in front of Sealer Robot #4, which had been implicated in a recent rash of water leaks. "How are we doing with sealer skips, Fred?"

"I think we've solved the problem, Tom. The filter had been getting clogged, so we've increased our maintenance frequency. No problems in the past week. We're watching it closely."

"Good work, Fred. Thanks." He was a good manager.

Then we went up to the mezzanine to have a look at our paint booths and bake ovens. Primer is applied first, then the colored topcoat, then a clear coat. Painted body units then go down to our inspection deck where we repair dirt, craters, ghosts, mars, fish-eyes and orange peel. Units with serious defects are sent to spot repair. If we can't fix it there, we have to repaint the unit.

Andy spent a lot of time watching spot repair and making notes in his little black book.

Back at the Paint team room he summarized what he had seen. Again, he was bang on. Freddie looked at me. How does he know all that?

"You're right, Mr. Saito," he said. "I'm looking forward to working with you."

Andy and I bid goodbye to Fred and followed the painted car body to our automatic storage and retrieval building (ASRB), a nine-level building, which can hold 600 vehicles. Some cars go directly into the Assembly department; others are held depending on the mix we need. When a car is needed, a crane extracts it from the tower.

The ASRB puts cars back into sequence. How do they get out of sequence? All the repair work we do. Without the ASRB we couldn't synchronize our production with that of our suppliers. Each week the head office gives us our build schedule: so many convertibles, so many hard tops, in these colors, with these options and in this order. Our suppliers get the same schedule and deliver accordingly. If we are out of sequence in assembly, it's chaos. Beige seats when we need gray seats, black bumpers when we need silver. The floor gets covered with seats, bumpers and instrument panels. This happens even with the ASRB. Without it we'd be sunk.

Andy saved his deepest frown for the ASRB. I added another item to my "Ask Andy" list.

The car is "stuffed" in the Assembly shop, which is five football fields long. There is also a mysterious mezzanine full of cobwebs and ancient equipment. Legend has it people live up there. It would be a great place for a phantom.

Our Assembly shop manager is Jeff Turner, a talented engineer who wears dress shirts and his hair slicked back like Michael Douglas in the film *Wall Street*. Jeff is torn between Sylvain and me. He's bright and ambitious and would like to follow Sylvain up the corporate ladder. But

Sylvain's arrogance and cruelty repel him. He'd like me to succeed but doesn't like my chances. Jeff's been in assembly for almost two years now and hasn't built anything. Maybe it's my fault. Have I taught him anything?

Assembly is full of parts and garbage: parts in front of each workstation; garbage everywhere else. We've launched countless housekeeping campaigns, to no avail. Andy stopped every few yards to pick up stuff. Jeff and I felt embarrassed so we did the same. We all eventually stopped; there was just too much of it.

We walked over to the trim lines where the process begins. We put the taillights on first. Then we remove the doors, which we reinstall after we've added window glass, hardware and trim. Next come the struts, instrument panel, windshield and back window. Then we install seats, bumpers, steering column, headliner and tires.

We stopped in front of the headlight install process at the end of Trim line 1. You could barely see behind all the parts. "Jeff-san," said Andy, "please explain why there are two days' worth of headlights here?"

"We've had quite a few part-outs here lately," Jeff replied. "I imagine the lift truck drivers want to make sure it doesn't happen again."

"How many part-outs do you have each day, Jeff-san?"

Jeff seemed uncomfortable. "I don't know. Our conveyance people would know."

Andy gestured to the pile of headlights. "Is this a normal or abnormal situation?"

"It's hard to say, sir."

"Correct, Jeff-san," he said gently. "How can one manage without a standard?"

We walked past the subassembly areas that feed the main line: door line, instrument panel and tire install. At the engine line, big V8s are hoisted onto a subframe and then raised into the car. We stood and watched for almost half an hour.

Andy drew out some of the walk patterns for us. "Pinball," he said.

Then he pointed out the tangle of tool cables above the work area. "Jungle gym."

Finally, he asked Jeff to unwrap the wire harnesses on process 4. "You have ten seconds."

It took Jeff 25 seconds—with the team member's help.

No wonder operators struggle to keep up. No wonder we ship garbage.

We finally arrived at the last two assembly processes: wheel alignment and water test. After these, Desperados were driven to our rail yard for delivery to a Taylor Motors dealership.

Andy, Jeff and I sat down at a table next to the line. Andy wanted to summarize what he had seen. I called Joe Grace on his cell phone and asked him to come over.

Joe is assistant plant manager and my right hand. He looks like a Zulu prince—coal-black eyes, gleaming skull and regal presence. Joe can reduce people to jelly with a cocked eyebrow. Until they get to know him and realize it's a put-on. A few years back we went to Japan together. We worked up a pretty good Muhammad Ali/Howard Cosell routine, which the Japanese loved. We've been pals ever since.

Joe is one of five brothers raised by a widowed father, a marine drill sergeant. His brothers include an accountant, a

lawyer, an engineer and an NBA player. Joe is the most disciplined person I've ever known. When I told him so, he
laughed. "You ought to see my dad."

"How did your dad do it?" I asked him once. "I mean,
turning out five boys like you all on his own?"

"My dad just said to us, 'Your name is Grace. You do not
get B's. You get A's.'"

"Hi, Mr. Saito," said Joe when he arrived. They had
already met.

"Seventeen of twenty processes we looked at in Assembly are incapable," Andy began. "Only six of twenty work-
stations had proper addresses. Only five of thirty-eight part
racks were properly labelled. Seventeen of thirty-eight part
racks had more than one day of inventory. Ten of thirty-
eight had more than two days' worth of inventory."

Andy continued like this for several minutes. Just the
facts. We listened quietly, with our heads down. Assembly
was our money department—where we got paid—and it
was a disaster.

Andy and I then walked over to the union office to meet
Carolyn West, the president of our local. As we walked I
summarized our vital statistics for Andy.

"We employ about three thousand people over two
eight-hour shifts and cover about two million square feet of
area. Our production target is four-hundred seventy units
per shift and nine-hundred forty units per day. We work
overtime every day and some Saturdays.

"We measure quality in terms of defects per one thousand. Our biggest problems are wrong or missing parts,

water leaks, chips and scratches, engine surges and stalls and body panel fit.

"Our main competitors are the Ford Mustang, GM Camaro and the Nissan Z series. We are way behind the best in class (Nissan). Luckily, Toyota isn't really into the muscle car market—yet."

Andy laughed.

Carolyn was waiting for us. She was an African-American who wore colorful hairpieces and rings on her face. She had survived a terrible marriage and had raised two girls on her own, both now in college. Carolyn put herself through school while working in Assembly. I was proud of her and of my company, which paid for her education.

I had told Carolyn about Andy. She knew the score.

After the introductions, Andy gave Carolyn the same report he had given to Jeff, Joe and me. She took it all in.

"So things are as bad as we thought."

"Much opportunity," said Andy. "But we will need your support."

"Mr. Saito," she said. "Tom Papas is the best thing that ever happened to us. We'd have lost this plant if not for him. If you're a friend of Tom's, then you're a friend of mine. If you need something from Carolyn, you just ask."

I didn't know what to say.

"That means a lot to me, Carolyn. Are you still going to give me a hard time in public?"

"Absolutely," she said, "just to keep my hand in."

Andy and I walked back in silence. We had work to do. Snow scrunched beneath our feet as we walked past the west docks. I counted twelve tractor-trailers unloading parts for the night shift. The plant seemed eerie in the darkness.

Back at the front office, Andy and I confirmed our schedule, shook hands and parted. I got into my car. Travon had repaired the parking lot gate.

But how long would it last?

Needs More Work

A ndy gave each department manager a summary of
what he had seen during our walkthrough. A week
later he wanted to see what we were doing about it. So I
asked that Antonio, Sylvain, Freddie and Jeff present their
strategic plans for the year, and that Joe Grace present our
overall strategy.

At Rachel Armstrong's insistence, the past few years
we've been trying policy deployment, or *hoshin kanri*, a
planning and execution system developed at Toyota. Every
December we identify breakthrough goals and develop
strategic plans. We spend the year fighting the usual fires
and at year-end hold a half-hearted review. We never do
what we said we'd do.

So here we are in the boardroom a week after our walkthrough. Threadbare furniture, coffee-stained carpets, Taylor logo not quite centered. It's a crummy February
morning. At least we have a shiny new roundtable. We can
hear the rattle of the Assembly shop. I have also invited our
extended management team: engineers, assistant managers, accountants, specialists from human resources,
finance, logistics and quality control.

Antonio, Sylvain, Freddie and Jeff make their presentations, one after another on the screen up front: multimedia PowerPoint slides and plenty of them.

Andy and I are at the front of the room. During Sylvain's presentation (47 slides) Andy gets up and walks to the drink table at the back. He gets a cold can of pop, returns to his chair and starts dabbing his forehead with it. He closes his eyes.

The lights come on. It's finally over, after three hours. I thank everyone and ask Andy for comments. He looks around the room. "Thank you very much for a good presentation. Much opportunity here." Then he gets up and walks out.

"Thanks everybody," I say and walk out after him. Sylvain follows us. He wants to know what Andy thinks of his strategy.

Andy looks at Sylvain. "Needs more work, John-san. Your strategy is not clear. Please reflect on last year. What were your targets? What was result of your activity? Where are the hot spots? What did you learn? What will you do differently?"

"But what do you think about my software, my engineering model?" Sylvain asks.

"Too academic. Body shop is not ready for advanced activities. Please focus on stability. Strengthen breakdown maintenance. Develop back-up for constraints. Involve team members. Solve problems. Basic, basic."

"Maybe you just don't *understand* it."

"Ah, maybe you teach me, John-san."

They eye one another.

"Good day, Mr. Saito," says Sylvain walking away. Andy looks over at me. "Much anger."

That night, Joe and I stayed very late to work out our next moves. We decided to start upstream in the Paint shop and then move quickly into Stamping and Body. If we could stabilize these areas, maybe we could quell the tidal wave of defects that was overwhelming Assembly.

We wanted some quick wins to generate momentum. But we also wanted to strengthen our overall strategy. We had both been embarrassed by the weakness of our strategic plans. We'd follow up with Andy on that one. I called Andy on his cell phone and shared our thinking. He said he was okay with it.

The next morning Andy and I met Fred and Joe in the Paint shop meeting room. Andy wanted quick action. "We must strengthen zone control! Plan, do, check and adjust; the Deming cycle. Each supervisor must grasp the situation in his zone and apply PDCA."

"Sounds good," said Fred. "How do we do that?"

"We will start with production analysis boards at metal repair. We will do pilot, confirm understanding and then expand to every zone. I will teach you, Fred-san. You teach supervisors."

Andy took a sheet of paper out of his old leather journal. "We will print out a large copy of this paper and post it on tripod next to metal repair booth. Every hour the supervisor will record results. At shift-end, the team will reflect. What did we learn?"

Production Analysis Board									
Area:			Date:		Supervisor:				
Hour	Production plan (hr/cum)	Actual production (hr/cum)	Variance	Offline repairs	Hourly top concerns	Downtime (seconds)			Reviewed by
						Blocked	Starved	Process	
1									
2									
3									
4									
5									
6									
7									
8									
9									
10									
Total									

Downtime codes:

Blocked = Downstream processes are full. We cannot make any more units.
Starved = Upstream processes are short. We have no units to work on.
Process = Process problems in our zone.

Top Three Problems	Countermeasures	Resp	Learning Points

We spent several minutes looking it over.

"Mr. Saito," Fred asked, "we already record some of this data in our computer system. Why do it again?"

"For visual management, Fred-san. The computer is a good tool, but only one person can see the screen. *Every* team member must be able to see the current condition. Do you know the visual management triangle?"

None of us had heard of it. Andy drew it out.

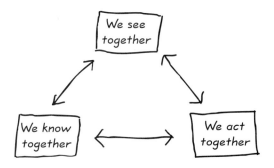

We mulled this one over, too. "It makes sense," Joe said.

Fred called Quincy, the metal repair team leader, on the radio and asked him to come over. When Quincy arrived Fred explained the purpose of the pilot and his responsibilities. Then he went over the PDCA cycle.

Quincy was okay with it. "No problem, boss"

We got together again at shift-end. Fred and Quincy called the metal repair team together, explained the purpose of the production analysis board pilot, their role and asked for questions. Again, there was no problem.

Then we did the same with the night shift team when they came in. Both shifts were on the same page; the pilot was ready to go.

Andy, Joe and I decided to go to the Iron Horse for dinner. Freddie took a rain check. It was past seven o'clock and already dark when we got there. An arctic wind cut through us. We hurried into the bar, found a booth and ordered Makers Mark all around. Joe had joined the bourbon club.

As usual, I was full of questions. "Saito-san, you looked unhappy during our strategy presentation yesterday."

"Yes," he said. "It had no meaning. The purpose of hoshin kanri is to identify most important needs and to develop strategy to achieve them. Hoshin kanri is PDCA for factory, department, section and team.

"The management team must grasp the situation! What were last year's results? What is the trend? Where are hot spots? What is condition of competitor? There was no reflection! How can you learn? You have no meaningful targets, no problem consciousness. Also, fifty pages for one plan are too much. Each strategy paper must be one page in the A3 format."

Andy scribbled on his napkin. "Hoshin kanri, or policy management, requires focus and alignment."

Before policy
management

After policy
management

Then he turned the napkin over and drew this one.

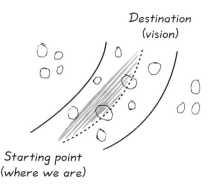

"What is the current condition? We must go and see. What is our vision? What are boulders and stones on the path? Grasp the situation! Then make a video."

"I don't understand sensei," Joe put in. "What do you mean by video?"

"A video is a set of pictures. Step one, step two, step three..."

"But life hardly ever goes according to plan," Joe said. "Why bother making a video, as you call it?"

"Good question, Joe-san. Who can answer it?" As I was learning, he never made it easy for us: He challenged us whenever he could.

"Well, as you said, a video is a set of pictures," I offered, "a story line, something to compare against ... a standard. That's it! A video is a standard."

"Good! Why do we need a standard?"

"Standards tell us how things should be," I continued. "Standards tell us when there is an abnormality."

"Yes!" Andy slapped the table with his hand. "Standards make the abnormality visible. We can begin to manage!"

His eyes were glowing coals. I could see how he built all those plants.

"Sensei, what does 'go and see' mean?" Joe asked.

"Managers must go and see actual conditions on the shop floor. Managers cannot depend on data alone, cannot depend on computers," he said, indirectly cuffing Sylvain.

I liked that. "What's an A3, sensei?"

Andy took a folded piece of paper out of his journal. "The A3 is Toyota's most important communication tool."

He unfolded an 11″ by 17″ sheet. It was a strategic plan for quality written years ago at Toyota UK. It told a clear, simple story. Here's what happened last year and what we learned. Here's what we need to do this year. Here is our rationale and our action plan.

We turned it over and found a summary of the plant's quality condition—16 charts each with a rating and an explanation. "A quality dashboard," he told us. I made a note to ask him about dashboards.

It was the clearest plan I had ever seen.

"Tom-san and Joe-san, I give you assignment. Please prepare strategy A3 for transformation of Desperado plant. Use this paper as a guide."

"Okay," said Joe. "But we'll be asking a lot of questions."

We ordered more drinks and some sandwiches. I knocked back the last of my bourbon. "Sensei, you talk a great deal about PDCA. Why is it so important?"

Focus: *Safety, Quality, Delivery…*

Title/Theme

Site/Dept.:

Last Year's Results/This Year's Targets/Mid-term Targets

This Year's Action Plan

Actions	Activity	Schedule
		J F M A M J J A S O N D

Reflection on Last Year's Activities

Activity	Rating	Key Results/Issues

Analysis/Justification to This Year's Activities

Follow-up/Unresolved Issues

Author: _____

Version # _____ Date: _____

Signatures					
Titles					

Andy took a sip of his drink. "PDCA is very easy to say. But it took me ten years to learn plan, ten years to learn do, ten for check and ten for adjust. Now I begin to understand PDCA.

"A manager must practice and teach PDCA! People believe Toyota system is tools: standardized work, 5S, kanban and so on. But most important is the thinking way!"

He took some paper out of his journal and drew it out.

"Understand?" he asked.

I thought about all the tools we had tried over the years that had fallen by the wayside. Every question he answered raised five more.

"Sensei, let's see if I get it. PDCA is the most important tool of management. Managers at every level must practice and teach PDCA. Hoshin kanri, or policy management, is PDCA at the plant level."

"Not just at the plant level," said Andy, "but also at the department, section and team level."

"Okay," I continued. "Are production analysis boards PDCA for supervisors?"

"Yes," Andy replied. "Frequency of check varies with management level. Senior managers check weekly, department managers check daily, team leaders check hourly and team members check each unit!"

"Mr. Saito, you're blowing my mind," Joe put in. "I see a series of concentric PDCA cycles."

Andy laughed. "Maybe too much bourbon, Joe-san! Next question: What is zone control?"

Joe handled that one. "Zone control means understanding inputs, outputs and the four M's through PDCA."

"Yes!" Andy replied. "The supervisor is like a small business owner. Sylvain-san has wrong thinking way. He should teach supervisors zone control."

It was sinking in. The Body shop's biggest problem was instability caused by the absence of zone control. Neither Sylvain nor his supervisors knew what was actually happening. He believed what the computers told him. The computers weren't bad in themselves, but they left too much out. I understood why we were starting with production analysis boards. We had to learn how to walk before we could run.

Dinner arrived. Joe had ordered the steak sandwich, Andy the Yukon burger. I bit into my BLT. Not bad, but my dad's was better. Even though there were still huge gaps in my understanding, I felt I was beginning to get it.

We had a chance.

Understanding Zone Control

I had a lot to think about the rest of the week. We continued our production analysis pilot in metal repair and made
plans to extend it across the Paint shop. There were still a lot
of questions Andy hadn't answered. Luckily, Dean Formica
was in town that weekend. I was especially happy to see him
because I knew he had knowledge I desperately needed.

We went to the Humpty Dumpty for lunch. March had
come in like a lamb, and the snow was melting. Dad was
delighted to see Dino.

"BUON GIORNO, DINO MY BOY. VIVA ITALIA!
MANGIATE MACARONI!"

"Hi, Mr. Nick," said Dean. Dad loved to show off his
Italian, such as it was. And he loved being called Mr. Nick.

"How is your father, my boy?"

"Everyone's great. Dad says hello."

Dean's dad was Giannino; his uncles were Pasqualino and
Giuseppino. We called them the Ino brothers. Like my parents, they had come from the old country as children after the
war. Mama and Mrs. Formica used to baby-sit for each other.
Mama says I could speak Italian when I was three. And Dino
can still speak some Greek, though not the nice words.

Mama heard Dad and came out saying "Nicky, that voice of yours…" Then she saw us and her face lit up. She came over and pinched our cheeks. "How are my boys?"

We settled into a booth and ordered souvlaki, Greek salad and cold beer. Mama brought out steaming spanakopita. She had made the filo herself.

"Good to see you, pal," I said. "How are your sisters Dina, Gina, Lina, Mina, Nina, Pina, Rina and Tina?"

He laughed. "They're fine. How about your sisters Koula, Noula, Soula, Toula and Voula?"

"They're good. And how are your brothers Gino, Lino, Mino, Nino, Pino, Rino and Tino?"

Our old shtick; we were both laughing.

I tried the spanakopita—incredible. "How goes Toyota Kentucky?"

"Our 550N launch is on track," Dean replied, "except for the spray robots. Our coverage is thin around the deck lid. We'll keep running trials till we get it right."

"Toyota always seems to be expanding, Dino. We haven't launched in a new plant in years."

He shrugged. "I'm working my butt off, but it is exciting. How's it going with Andy?"

"He's great. I'm beginning to understand where we are, and where we need to be. But it's a quantum leap, and I don't know if we can handle it. We showed Andy our strategic plans last week. You should've seen his face."

"Did he do his Coke-can-to-the-forehead routine?"

"Yeah, it was pretty embarrassing," I admitted. "We don't know how to plan or execute. Hell, we don't know how to manage. All we do is talk."

"Don't be too hard on yourselves. It took us years in Kentucky. And we had Andy and many other senseis. It was mechanical at first. Understanding came gradually."

"We're starting slowly," I said. "Andy is teaching us plan-do-check-adjust. We're using production analysis boards."

Dino laughed. "Zone control! When we first launched, our coaches forced us to use those damn things. It took me a while to get it. Production analysis boards help you understand your zone. Then you develop countermeasures for common problems, which you sustain through redundant checking. Managers check group leaders, who check team leaders and so on. Imagine concentric circles."

He drew it out on a napkin.

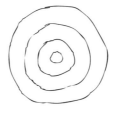

"Each circle represents a PDCA cycle. Now imagine that each check is 90 percent effective. The reliability of the system is given by the formula: $R = 1-(1-0.9)^n$, where n is the number of PDCA cycles.

"Do the math. If you have five PDCA cycles, only ten defects per million reach the customer. But at Toyota Kentucky, we have more than five PDCA cycles—and the effectiveness is better than 90 percent."

"So that's how you win all those quality awards."

"In Kentucky," he continued, "we built our activities slowly, based on need. Thirteen years later, we have an advanced system. But you should see Tsutsumi, our mother plant. They've had an extra twenty years and it shows. It keeps you humble. Someone is always better."

I took another piece of spanakopita. "Do you still use production analysis boards?"

Dean took a piece too. "Of course we do. We've augmented them with software and other stuff. But software can't replace problem consciousness. We want managers on the shop floor, not sitting in front of computers."

Mama brought us souvlaki; lamb for me, pork for Dean. I poured olive oil and red wine vinegar onto my bread plate. "Tell me more about zone control."

Dean took a swig of his beer. "Zone control means understanding inputs and outputs to your zone. Your supplier is the previous zone, your customer the next zone. You communicate upstream, downstream and between shifts."

Dean drew it out on another napkin. "I swear you learn more from pub and dinner napkins than you ever learned at college," he said.

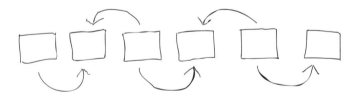

"You develop simple processes. Better yet, you ask your team members to develop them. Then you standardize everything and make it visible. You come to realize involvement is the key. In Kentucky, our team members check *every car*. So you ask, 'What skills do we need? What standards do we need? How do we make them visible?' And you build support systems."

My brain was doing the bossa nova.

"Sorry for running on. I love this stuff, but I don't want to overload you. Feel free to call whenever you need to."

"I don't mind, Dino. It's such a different way of thinking. But something's bothering me. It took years to build the systems at Toyota Kentucky. We have ten months. Do you think we have a chance?"

"If the management team and the union are aligned, you can make big gains in a short time," Dean replied. "But you won't become Toyota unless you sustain it over the long term."

Dean paused. "But we haven't talked about you. What's happening with Teal and the children?"

"Sometimes she lets me see the girls, sometimes not," I said. "My lawyer is appealing to the courts. I can't understand why she's doing this."

"Do you think she wants you back? I always thought she was crazy about you."

"I don't know. But I couldn't go back, Dean. Too much water under the bridge."

We sat there drinking beer, mulling over this simple truth. I was still curious about Andy's background so I took the opportunity to see if Dean knew anything else that might enlighten me.

"Dino, why did Andy drop out? Why is he living in Jersey of all places? Is there a Mrs. Saito?"

"I'm not sure why he dropped out. I have *no* idea why he's living in Jersey. There certainly *was* a Mrs. Saito. She was a great lady, and you could tell there was a strong feeling between them. I remember once Andy got drunk at our Christmas party. He was really jovial and funny, but he was falling down. Such things don't embarrass the Japanese.

"And I said, 'Mrs. Saito, what should we do with him?' And she said, 'Oh he's a silly man. Please clean him up and help me take him home.'"

Then we heard that she wasn't well. Andy started taking time off—something he never did. He even showed up to work drunk a few times. Nobody could understand what was happening. He was always so disciplined and so inspiring. He was our leader.

"Then Andy took a leave of absence. We didn't know if Mrs. Saito's condition had worsened or if Andy himself had gotten sick. Then he just disappeared. That was over two years ago. It's a terrible thing to see someone you admire fall apart like that."

"I almost fell apart, Dean."

"I know, Tommy. We were all worried about you. Thank God you survived. But you know, I think it's time you got out a bit. The plant and the girls are your whole life."

"Now that you mention it, I've got the band back together. We're playing this Saturday at the Blue Giraffe. Why don't you come along?"

"Glad to hear you're playing again, Tom. Sure, I'll come Saturday, but on one condition: No questions about zone control."

At this point my Uncle Angie sauntered over. "My boys, I just wanted to say hello."

"Good to see you, Angie," said Dino. "You still playing the clarinet?"

"Dino, it's the best instrument. When I play you should see them dance! But I want to ask you for a favor." Angie made a face in my direction. "Can you get me a deal on a *Camry*?"

"Get out of here, you bum," I told him.

Time Out at the Blue Giraffe

Whenever I can, I play in a band at the Blue Giraffe in Hoboken. Our bass player knows the owner. I have a wine-red Stratocaster and a 1962 Fender Tweed Blues amp. I play the harmonica in a rack like Jimmy Reed. On gig days I feel like I'm in an Elvis movie—welder by day, rock singer by night.

My playing has never been better. Being screwed up gives you soul, I guess. Once after an over-the-top set, Sidney the barkeep shook his head. "Where did a Greek boy learn to play the blues like *that?*"

"Greek people have been playing the blues for three thousand years," I told him. "As a matter of fact, the first blues player was a Greek boy. His name was Homer and he was blind."

"Where *do* you come up with this stuff?"

It's Saturday night about nine o'clock. Dean decided to come along to keep me company. We're having a drink with the band before the first set. Johnny, an Aussie investment banker, plays the bass. Tony, a Jersey City cop, plays lead guitar on a beautiful Sunburst Les Paul. Jeffrey, an African-

American CFO, is our drummer. Tony is busting Johnny's chops, as only a Jersey cop can. The rest of us are laughing at the glorious nonsense.

We play classic blues and R&B with some of my stuff thrown in. If the stars and moon are aligned, we sound pretty good. If they aren't, we sound like the metal repair bay at the plant.

The place is packed and we've got butterflies. What if we suck?

The lights go out. We walk to the small stage and take out our instruments. Sidney, who has taken off his apron, hollers into the mike. "And now the moment we've all been waiting for. Put your hands together for the Ayatollah of Rock'n Rollah, the Thunder from Down Under, the Hardest Working Man in the Jersey City police department, and the CFO from the UFO! TOM PAPAS AND THE BLUES DISCIPLES!!!!!"

We hit the first chord. I pull what I hope are searing notes out of my harp as Tony's guitar wails behind me. Jeff and Johnny are laying down a solid rhythm. Little Walter's *Blues with a Feeling*—always a crowd pleaser.

Blues with a feelin', that's what I had today
I'm gonna find my baby if it takes all night and day.

We relax. It's going to be a good night.

There are three attractive women sitting at a table near the stage. The girl on the right is looking at me. Mama mia, she's cute. Her two friends walk over to the dance floor, which is filling up. She sits there taking in the music. I want to protect her, sitting there all by herself.

We end the set with *I Heard It Through the Grapevine*, one of my all-time faves. I whisper into the mike, "We're gonna take a little break now. But don't you go away 'cause we'll be playing for you *all night long.*"

Back at the table Dean is giving us high fives. "You guys aren't as bad as I thought. Guess I won't need my ear plugs after all." We order beers all around, and bask in the goofy glow.

Dean leans over and whispers, "Did you see that woman checking you out?"

"She's beautiful," I say. "My heart skips a beat when I look at her."

"She is *into* you, man. Go over and talk to her."

"I can't Dino. I mean I want to, but I'm so screwed up, I wouldn't know what to say."

"Get your ass over there."

"I can't. I just can't do it."

"All right then. *I'll* do it." Dino walks over to the table with the three women. He chats them up, looks over at me and makes a 'he's hopeless' gesture. They are laughing; my girl looks over at me and smiles.

I smile back and make a 'can I buy you a drink?' gesture. She nods—Yes! A minute later we are sitting together at the bar.

Her name is Sarah. Almond eyes, delicate cheekbones, tawny blond curls to her shoulders. She is wearing a red cotton dress and just the right amount of blush. "I got it in Crete," she says. She means the dress.

"It's a beautiful place," I tell her. "My family is from Corfu." We talk about Greece for a while.

She's thirty-one, the youngest of three children. She teaches second grade in the city and shares a loft in Hoboken with her two friends. Her parents were Hungarian refugees who fled the Soviet tanks in 1956 and met in New York. Lots of suffering, like my folks. She exudes kindness. She is into things Chinese and Japanese. When she laughs her face lights up like a little girl's.

I tell her about my folks, my girls and our plant.

"I like the way you sing," she says.

"Like a circular saw cutting through a cedar plank..."

She laughs. "No, really, it gets to people. My friends were saying the same thing. That man can sing."

I tell her about Homer and do my impersonation of Sidney the barkeep.

She laughs again and my God, she is glowing. She is glowing. Either she's radioactive or she likes me. I sure like her.

"You look like a cross between Robert DeNiro and Sean Penn," she says.

"Worst of both?"

"No, best of both."

"You look like an angel," I tell her.

We sit together like that, enjoying the warmth, comfort, attraction.

Dino nudges me. "Wake up, Casanova." It takes a moment.

"Sarah, it's time for the next set. Will you stay for a while?"

"Well, I have an early day tomorrow. We'll stay for a little while."

"Can I call you?" I ask.

"How about I call you?"

I write my phone number on the back of my business card, pang in my heart. Then I rejoin the boys up on the little stage. Before I hit the first note I look over at Sarah and mouth the words, "Please call me."

She smiled—and she did.

Making Our Video

At our first cool-down at the Iron Horse, after the horrid PowerPoint presentations, Andy had given Joe and me an assignment: To develop a strategic plan for the transformation of New Jersey Motor Manufacturing.

He had pointed out all our planning weaknesses. We had not grasped our current situation; we didn't know where we were going or what obstacles lay in our path. He had said we needed to make a video (i.e., a set of clear, simple pictures), which would show the path forward and help make abnormalities visible.

So the following week Joe and I set up a brainstorming session with the extended management team, meaning Antonio, Fred, John and Jeff, as well as middle managers, engineers and specialists from finance, human resources, quality control, logistics and other supporting departments.

Anne booked our ratty conference room for the whole day and arranged for breakfast and lunch. It was a sloppy March morning—snow, slush and a damp wind. We were all sick of winter.

People looked out-of-it as they arrived. It wasn't just the winter blues. What are we doing here? they were wondering.

I poured myself a cup of java and kicked off the session.

"Welcome to our brainstorming session. You all know the senior management team—Joe Grace, Antonio Villareal, Fred Henderson, John Sylvain and Jeff Turner. I'd also like to introduce Mr. Andy Saito, our friend and mentor.

"To build our future we have to get better at planning and execution. We need to develop clear objectives and a good strategy. That's what we'll do today—and every year from now on.

"Please turn off your radios, pagers and cell phones. I need each of you to get involved. There are no bad ideas, no wrong answers. Please make this your plan. So let's get started."

I drew Andy's road image on the whiteboard. "What's our current condition? In other words, where are we now?"

Shrugs, scowls and blank stares.

"We really don't know, do we?" I went on. "That's one of our problems. We need to get better at measurement. To get us started, I asked Antonio to put together our plant's latest safety, quality, delivery and cost results."

Antonio went through a series of slides. It wasn't pretty.

"So that's where we are," I said when Antonio had finished. "Now, where do we *need* to go?"

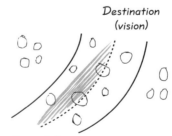

Destination
(vision)

Starting point
(where we are)

More blank stares; they had never been asked before. So I wrote this year's goals on the whiteboard:

- 20 percent improvement in our main safety, quality, delivery and cost indicators.
- 25 percent reduction in ergonomic burden.[1]

"If we meet these goals, the head office will take notice, I promise you. But are these the only goals?"

Someone piped up. "Tom, I think we also have a long-term goal. We have to implement the Toyota Production System. Otherwise, we'll be back in the soup next year."

There were murmurs of agreement.

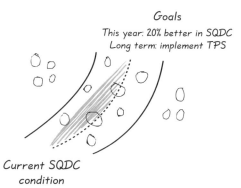

I wrote it down. "Thank you. So here are the goals for this year and for the longer term."

These were baby steps, but we had never taken them before.

---

1. Ergonomic burden reflects physical burden and comprises the combined effects on the human body of muscle force, repetition, posture and environmental conditions.

"Now I'd like you to break up into four groups. Identify and discuss what you feel are our biggest obstacles—our boulders. Be ready to report out in thirty minutes."

Andy, Joe and I wandered from group to group. "Just listen," Andy had advised, and that's what we did. After some initial discomfort, people got into it. Pretty soon they were singing like canaries.

The consensus was that our biggest obstacles were:

- No time—we were too busy running to breakdowns to develop any management systems.
- Incapable processes—most of our production processes could not be done correctly within cycle time; our administrative processes were also broken. So people took shortcuts.
- Machine instability—which led to a fire-fighting mentality.
- Weak standards—we didn't really know what should be happening with respect to the four M's: man and woman, method, material and machines, or with respect to safety, quality, delivery or cost.
- Weak visual management—you couldn't tell what was happening at a glance anywhere in the plant.
- No involvement of shop floor workers–for years our unofficial motto had been, "Check your mind at the door."

- Perverse accounting measures—for example, we were rewarded for shipping junk.

We had free-wheeling discussions about each obstacle. People began to enjoy themselves. The genie of involvement was out of the bottle. Why hadn't I done this before?

"Good work everyone," I told them. "Now we know where we are, where we need to be and the obstacles in our path. Let's take a ten-minute pit stop. When we come back, Mr. Saito will show us how to 'make the video,' as he calls it."

After the break Andy passed out a strategic planning A3 template.

"We have enough information to complete the left side of A3 paper—the goals and reflection on last year," he told us. "Now we need the action plan. Please understand, the point is not the paper. What is the point?"

"The thinking is the point!" someone sang out.

Andy took us through a simple example called 'Becoming a Good Swimmer,' which taught us how to turn our objectives into an action plan. In small groups we developed affinity and tree diagrams, which many of us had used before.

   We filled the walls with sticky notes and then organized
the ideas into meaningful piles. Here is one group's work.

Becoming a good swimmer

Becoming a good swimmer

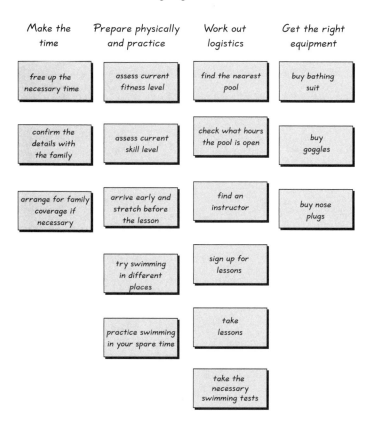

Make the time	Prepare physically and practice	Work out logistics	Get the right equipment
free up the necessary time	assess current fitness level	find the nearest pool	buy bathing suit
confirm the details with the family	assess current skill level	check what hours the pool is open	buy goggles
arrange for family coverage if necessary	arrive early and stretch before the lesson	find an instructor	buy nose plugs
	try swimming in different places	sign up for lessons	
	practice swimming in your spare time	take lessons	
		take the necessary swimming tests	

From these we developed our tree diagrams.

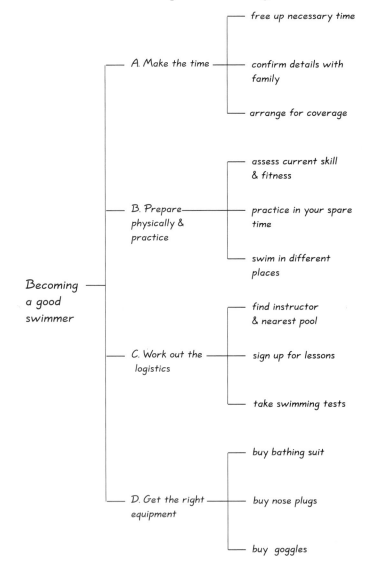

We had fun. I let them finish and called for another break.

When they returned, it was time for the real thing.

"Now let's develop a strategy to transform New Jersey Motor Manufacturing."

We had false starts and went into blind alleys. We filled the walls with ideas, which we grouped and regrouped. When we were happy with the upper branches of the tree, we broke up into smaller groups and worked on the lower branches.

Lunch came and went. Through the grimy windows we saw snow falling. It would be a long drive home. We stuck with it till we nailed it. Here is the seventh draft of our tree diagram, from which we developed our A3 strategy [see next page].

It was getting dark outside. We took another break.

When we resumed, I gave everyone a basic Toyota Production System text and the following images, which I had gotten out of one of Andy's textbooks.[3]

"These pictures [page 79] summarize the Toyota Production System," I told them. "Our strategy is clear: Leaders must teach TPS. So let's get started."

There was a good deal of chirping. "You mean we're starting right away?" someone called out.

"Yup," I said. "I'd like each manager to pick a topic. Managers will teach one another. Then we'll teach our

---

3. For a detailed discussion of these images please refer to *Lean Production Simplified: A Plain Language Guide to the World's Most Powerful Production System* (Productivity Press, 2002) by Pascal Dennis.

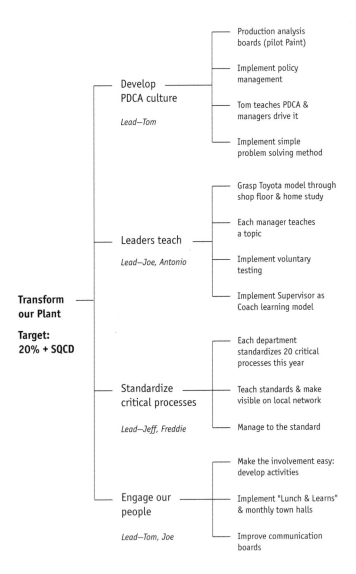

Transform
our Plant

Target:
20% + SQCD

Develop
PDCA culture

Lead—Tom

- Production analysis boards (pilot Paint)
- Implement policy management
- Tom teaches PDCA & managers drive it
- Implement simple problem solving method

Leaders teach

Lead—Joe, Antonio

- Grasp Toyota model through shop floor & home study
- Each manager teaches a topic
- Implement voluntary testing
- Implement Supervisor as Coach learning model

Standardize
critical processes

Lead—Jeff, Freddie

- Each department standardizes 20 critical processes this year
- Teach standards & make visible on local network
- Manage to the standard

Engage our
people

Lead—Tom, Joe

- Make the involvement easy: develop activities
- Implement "Lunch & Learns" & monthly town halls
- Improve communication boards

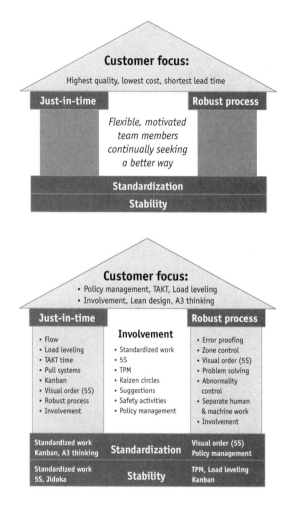

direct reports, who will teach their direct reports and so on. Everyone talks about 'learning organizations.' So let's just do it."

I volunteered to teach PDCA and policy management. Other senior managers chipped in and soon we had our curriculum:

- Plan-do-check-adjust and policy management—Tom Papas.
- Visual management and the 5S system—Joe Grace.
- Quick changeover and pull systems—Antonio Villareal.
- Just-in-time—Jeff Turner.
- Error-proofing—Fred Henderson.
- Total productive maintenance—John Sylvain.

I looked around the room. It was almost 7:00 P.M., and the team was exhausted. It was cold and dark outside. At least it had stopped snowing.

"That's a wrap. Sorry for keeping you late. Good work today. Drive safely."

I invited the senior managers to the Iron Horse for dinner, but even they were too tired. So Andy and I drove over, went in and settled into our usual booth. The bartender made a fuss when she saw us and sent over a couple of drinks. It was getting to feel like home.

We touched glasses. Kampai.

"How'd we do today, sensei?"

"Strategy is okay. Good leadership, Tom-san. But transformation is very difficult."

"My head hurts," I told him.

"Mine, too," he said, "but we are not finished. Do you know Fukuda's parable?"

"Never heard of it, sensei. Who is Fukuda?"

"Fukuda-san is a great sensei, a master of strategy. He has developed an image to help us understand transformation."

Andy pulled a sheet out of his journal and drew it out for me.

"Change is a voyage, Tom-san. But only about ten percent understand the need and want to be rowers. Most people don't understand the need for change. They are watchers. A few, maybe ten percent, are opposed to change. The grumblers will resist change.

"We need to understand who are the rowers, watchers and grumblers. We must support the rowers and ignore the grumblers, unless they become destructive. Over time, if our plan is good, the watchers will become rowers."

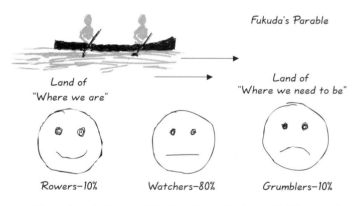

Fukuda's Parable

Land of "Where we are"

Land of "Where we need to be"

Rowers—10%   Watchers—80%   Grumblers—10%

We ordered dinner. My head really hurt. I felt hourly team members would support our plan. If we succeeded, their lives would be better.

Would middle management—assistant managers, engineers, specialists and supervisors—support us? Engaging team members meant giving up control.

Would senior managers accept the leader-as-teacher concept? I felt they would, except for Sylvain and possibly Jeff.

Sylvain was the only obvious grumbler. He didn't believe TPS would work in our plant or that leaders should teach. Or that team members could contribute. He thought PDCA was trivial. "We already do this, Tom," he said to me last week. "It's pretty basic."

I looked at him. "Then why do you make so much garbage? Our scrap yard is full of it."

Sylvain smiled, "I'll try to do better, Tom."

He was pretty sure of himself, given his connection to Jed Morgan and the Taylor family. He didn't think I could touch him.

Sylvain was a classic Taylor manager. *My shop is my kingdom. Thou shalt do as I say.* He didn't want team members solving problems. That was the engineer's job. He only went to the floor to beat people up. Sylvain didn't like Andy, or me, for that matter.

And I didn't like Sylvain—his glibness and arrogance, the way he treated people. It meant nothing to him if we lost the plant. Taylor Motors had 130 factories around the world—40 in North America alone. Sylvain knew he was going to be a plant manager and eventually a vice president. He could not imagine that Taylor Motors could be eclipsed by the Japanese.

Andy always emphasized the "three C's": consideration, communication and cooperation. Sylvain had the "three A's:" arrogance, anger and abuse—as we were soon reminded.

Kick-Off

A few days later I gave Bill Barrett a progress report. "Our production analysis board pilot in Paint went well. Now we're rolling it out across the shop. The management team is aligned and focused. We've put together a good strategy. Tomorrow we're having a town hall meeting to kick it off. We have a real shot at turning this place around. My biggest worry is Sylvain."

"I understand, Tom. He's been a thorn in your side for a long time. But we have to handle him with kid gloves. I can't fire him. He's married to Peggy Taylor; he's Jed Morgan's protégé. Please don't do anything without talking to me."

Then I called Dean Formica. "Sounds like a cement-head, Tom. Some people never get this stuff. Don't waste your time."

"But I can't fire him. He's married to Alfred Taylor's great-granddaughter."

"You don't have to fire him," Dino said. "Take over his responsibilities. Eventually, he may leave on his own."

"Dino, I think you may be on to something. Say, do you have cement-heads at Toyota?"

"Not many, Tom. Our hiring process is pretty robust."

"At Taylor Motors, we use the Pulse Test," I said. "If you've got one, you're hired."

Dino laughed. "People have this misconception that Toyota people are brilliant. It's not true. Do you want to know the biggest difference between Taylor Motors and Toyota? Taylor has brilliant people working broken processes and achieving mediocre results. Toyota has regular people working excellent processes and achieving excellent results."

"Does Toyota get rid of cement-heads?"

"Not usually. When it comes to people, the Japanese are eternal optimists. They believe everyone can improve so we keep working our deadbeats. And you know, we've turned a lot of them around."

The following day we held our town hall meeting. I had asked Anne to invite all our team members–almost three thousand people and to arrange for coffee, donuts and fruit. To make sure everyone could attend, we decided to hold it between shifts, in our cavernous Assembly shop. The last time we had met here was five years ago to celebrate our gold medal for quality. It seemed so long ago.

The place was buzzing. There was sound system feedback as the technicians completed their tests. It was odd to see the assembly line motionless, cars, tools and parts all around.

Carolyn West, our union president, whispered, "Good luck," and walked to the microphone. She welcomed everybody, did the introductions and called my name.

I looked out over the sea of faces. These were people I cared about, whose livelihoods depended on the course we were taking.

"A lot of people believe we're finished," I began. "They've read the papers, heard the rumors. I don't like that kind of talk. We will save our plant beyond *any* possibility of doubt. If anyone doubts this, let him leave now.

"We've put together a great plan. We're all going back to school. We're going to learn the Toyota Production System. Mr. Andy Saito is going to help us. We're going to communicate with you like never before. We're going to attack problems like never before.

"But I need each of you to get involved. I need each of you to make problems visible and to help fix them. I need each of you to figure out safer and better ways to do the work. I need you to feel 'this is *my* machine, *my* team and *my* plant.'"

I went on like this for several minutes, really feeling it. When I finished there was absolute silence, and then a roar of approval. We unveiled a banner that read *Take Action to Build Our Future*. I signed it and asked everyone to come up and do the same. It would be hung in our main entrance.

Carolyn and I went out into the crowd. Handshakes, high-fives and backslaps. Curtis, a 30-year veteran embraced me. "We gonna save this plant, my brother."

"You're goddamn right we are, Curt."

Clarence, our final line team leader, came over and put his arm around me. "Tommy, you got your mojo working now!"

But I knew just how quickly that mojo could disappear. As I drove home that night, I noticed that some idiot had driven through the parking lot gate again.

Big Heart

We began to get stronger. By night we were reading about TPS, by day we were practicing what we'd read. Spending 12 hours a day with Andy helped. Our days usually ended at the Iron Horse, sipping Makers Mark and shooting the breeze. Joe, Antonio and other managers often joined us—everyone but Sylvain.

By the end of March, I had my old energy back. Andy was getting stronger too. I felt good when he was around. One night, sitting in the Iron Horse, I told him about my parents. How they had come to this country with nothing. How proud I was of them, and of America.

I remembered that my folks wanted to meet Andy and had asked me to invite him for dinner. "I am going to make melonocarouna and gourabiedes," Mama had said. "I am going to make my best moussaka for this nice man who is helping my son."

"AND I'M GOING TO ORDER THE FRESHEST LAMB FROM SPIRO, MY IDIOT BROTHER. PFFT, I SPIT IN HIS DIRECTION!" said Dad.

"Nicky, you love Spiro. He didn't shortchange you. You counted wrong."

"NOULA, DON'T START WITH ME NOW. I KNOW WHAT I SAW."

Little Sophie ran over laughing and jumped into his lap. "Pappou, you're too noisy!"

"You hear that, Tommy? That's your mother for you. Too noisy she says. NOULA, WHAT ARE YOU SAYING TO THE CHILDREN?"

My beautiful, logical Helen chimed in, "It's not Yiayia's fault, Pappou. You just have a very loud voice."

I smiled at the memory. I extended my parents' invitation to Andy.

Andy's face lit up. "Thank you, Tom-san. I would be happy to come. We will find a time."

And for the first time, I told him about my ex-wife. Not everything, just that I was having problems. I didn't feel it was right to spill my guts.

"I am sorry, Tom-san," he said. "Some problems have no solution. One day they just go away. But you must never give up. You must have a *big* heart." He made a gesture: a heart growing in his chest.

Big heart. I liked that. I wondered whether anything was left of my heart.

"It's just torn up," Sarah had said. "We can put it back together."

We were walking along the waterfront, looking at the city across the river.

"I'm a spaceship," I told her.

"I know. A spaceship with a torn up heart. The worst kind." This is my kind of girl, I thought.

Then I was back in the Iron Horse with Andy.

"Life is about standards," he said, "values."

On the surface he was relaxed, flexible—suggesting, rarely insisting. But his core was polished steel. I remembered Chiba-sensei at our old aikido dojo telling us about the Forty-Seven Ronin, the renegade samurai who had also remained true to their values.

"Chiba-sensei always talked about values."

"Chiba-sensei has a big heart." Andy smiled. "What are your values, Tom-san?"

I laughed. "You're always challenging me. I need a drink before answering that one."

I took a long pull on my beer.

"Family, team, community, simple decency, good cars at fair prices, decent jobs . . ."

We sat in silence.

"How about you, sensei?"

He laughed.

"Open mind, teamwork, challenge! That was my motto for many years. To take care of our team members and community. To improve every day and never give up! We built many plants, developed strong teams and made good cars!

"Now I have added one more—but too late."

"What is that, sensei?"

"Family."

I wanted to ask him about his family. I wanted to know what had happened to him. But he was my sensei. He would tell me when he was ready.

The Money Board

We kept getting stronger. By mid-April our weekly management meeting had become a PDCA meeting. I drove Antonio, Freddie, Sylvain and Jeff hard. I put a lot of heat on Joe Grace.

"Where are the hot spots? What are you doing about them?"

To help answer these questions I asked Joe to implement daily process reviews. These were held on the shop floor every day at 1:00 P.M. on a rotating basis in each shop. The extended management team was invited. We went to the actual hot spot where the presenter told a PDCA story using a standard A3 template.

There were logistical problems. The plant was huge and noisy. So Joe put whiteboards on wheels and purchased cordless microphones and portable speakers.

Word got out that Joe and I always attended; pretty soon it was the thing to do after lunch. It got managers, engineers and specialists from every department out on the floor where they belonged. Joe and I encouraged freewheeling debate. We even gave it a name: "shooting the breeze." There was a lot of cross-fertilization and learning.

Antonio, Freddie, Sylvain, Jeff, Joe and I did "lunch and learns" across the plant: Supervisors got a lunch and a Toyota Production System lesson. Then they gave the same lesson to their team members. Our cafeteria got a lot of business. By teaching, we learned. By going to see, we confirmed what we had learned.

Something marvelous began to happen. My PDCA cycle compelled PDCA in my direct reports, which compelled PDCA in theirs. It was like a series of gears.

Freddie led the way in the Paint shop. Supervisors and team members had developed a basic grasp of zone control. We had production analysis boards in all zones now. Here is one from the sealer line.

Production Analysis Board									
Area: **Sealer Deck**				Date: **April 27**		Supervisor: **Bill Henry**			
Hour	Production plan (hr/cum)	Actual production (hr/cum)	Variance	Offline repairs	Hourly top concerns	Downtime (minutes)			Reviewed by
						Blocked	Starved	Process	
1	60/60	50/50	10	0	Sealer skips, robot 2		2	8	BH
2	60/120	60/110	0	0					BH
3	60/180	55/165	5	1	Overspray, smears			5	BH
4	60/240	50/215	10	3	Overspray, sealer skips, body down		3	7	BH
5	60/300	60/275	0	0					BH
6	60/360	45/320	15	4	Overspray, prime booth down	8		3	BH
7	60/420	55/375	5	0	Body down		5		BH
8	60/480	60/435	0	0					BH
9		45/480							
10									
Total	480	480							

Downtime codes:

Blocked = Downstream processes are full. We cannot make any more units.
Starved = Upstream processes are short. We have no units to work on.
Process = Process problems in our zone.

At a glance, anybody could tell how the team had done that day, and what they needed to work on.

Then we launched in Stamping, Body and Assembly with the help of Antonio, Sylvain and Jeff, respectively. The launches went smoothly in every shop except Body. As I said, Sylvain didn't believe in PDCA or that supervisors or team members should be involved.

It was a beautiful morning, and I was giving Andy a progress report. We sat in my dilapidated office. Blue sky filled the window. The warm sun and abundant rain had awakened the earth. In the distance we could see the Manhattan skyline.

Andy was generally pleased with our progress. "The first steps were the most difficult. We are now ready to pilot a 'money board' at Paint final line."

A money board, he explained, is essentially a production analysis board at the final process in a department or plant. That was where you got paid—hence the name. Money boards summarized each zone's hourly results and measured first time through, the most basic measure of quality. Quality wouldn't improve until we understood FTT.

FTT entails measuring all backflows:

$$FTT = \left(\begin{array}{c} \text{Total cars} - \text{repaints} - \text{spot repairs} - \\ \text{parts changes} - \text{other backflows} \end{array} \right) \div (\text{Total cars})$$

We paid little attention to it.

"What is the current FTT in the Paint shop?" Andy asked.

"Ninety percent according to our production report," I replied.

He looked at me like I had two heads. "Let's go and see."

I called Freddie on his cell phone and asked him to pull together his FTT data and to meet us at the Paint final line.

We decided to walk outside. We passed the scrap yard where a tractor was piling shiny car bodies into long metal bins. Andy didn't have to say anything. Talk about visual management.

As we passed the automatic storage and retrieval building, I realized how foolish my earlier statement had been. The nine-story ASRB existed to fix our shattered sequence. How could our FTT possibly be 90 percent?

Freddie was waiting for us at the Paint final line. He was embarrassed: Our FTT wasn't 90 percent—it was 57 percent. We had only been measuring *repaints*, and not spot repairs, parts changes or other backflows. "I apologize, Tom," he told me.

"No need to apologize, Freddie. I'm as much to blame."

I was also embarrassed. We did things wrong 43 percent of the time. What if pilots or surgeons had that kind of failure rate? How could we be so bad? No wonder we were losing money.

Andy emphasized "grasping the situation." We were taking a painful step.

I asked Freddie to pilot a money board ASAP.

Over the next few days Fred, Joe and I put our heads together. Why all the backflows? We looked upstream. Freddie walked the floor every day, listening and coaching. He introduced 10-minute pre- and post-shift meetings at the money board with his supervisors, engineers and specialists. Fred followed a set agenda:

- What are the biggest problems in your zone?
- What are you doing about them?
- What help do you need?

Problems began to surface. Some were easy to fix; others weren't. As I expected, some engineers, specialists and supervisors resisted. They didn't like zone control, because they couldn't hide their problems and they couldn't blame their team members. They had to *own* their problems. "Go see" was a shock for some. The shop floor is intense and full of problems. Freddie had frank discussions with several people. I let a few of them go. Word got around. And the Paint shop got stronger.

We hit the "no time" obstacle next. Andy had taught us to "go and see," but all we seemed to do was attend meetings. I suspected that most of these were status reports. We needed to free up time for value-added meetings like process reviews and lunch and learns. So I asked Antonio to set up a working group to assess our current condition and to develop a plan to free up time.

Antonio's team found that the extended management team spent almost 80 percent of its time in meetings and that half of this time was wasted. They came up with the following guidelines:

- Daily meeting time—no more than 50 percent.
- Shop floor time—at least 20 percent.

Antonio and the team also developed guidelines for:

- When to have a meeting and when *not* to.
- Meeting length (target: 25 minutes; max: 55 minutes).
- How to create an agenda.
- How to lead a meeting.

Antonio's team taught the standard through a series of lunch and learns. They posted it in all meeting rooms and gave pocket-sized laminated copies to everyone. They tracked progress using our meeting management software. As I had suspected, many meetings were status reports for the head office. I showed the data to Bill and asked him to filter reporting demands. He agreed.

Basic stuff, but a breakthrough for us.

We gathered momentum. Now that supervisors had data and time, they could communicate upstream and downstream. Zone control blossomed. Our safety, quality, delivery and cost results started to improve.

Working late in the Paint shop one night we saw streaks on the left fender coming into Zone B. Each unit would have to be repainted. Eddie Johnson, the supervisor, is a round African-American with a voice like Wilson Pickett. He set up containment and called Tracy, his counterpart in Zone A.

"We've got streaks on the left side fender again, Tracy. Seven last hour and eight the hour before. Did you change the wipe down process?"

"Yes we did Eddie," Tracy replied. "We're mixing our own solvent instead of using the presoaked cloth. It's a cost saving."

"Is that really a cost saving? Do me a favor. For the next hour, use the presoaked cloth. Put a marker on each car and let's see what happens."

"All right," said Tracy.

When we returned the streaks had disappeared. Tracy said they'd use presoaked rags from now on.

"Good thinking, Eddie-san," said Andy. "SQDC—everything is connected. Thank you for the good checking. Please continue."

Eddie was grinning like a Motown crocodile. Then we went down to see Tracy. "Anything we can do to make sure we don't get streaks again?" I asked.

I knew what I wanted—amend the standardized work, retrain operators on both shifts and put in a visual aid. In the past, I would have simply told Tracy what to do. I think she was expecting to catch hell. I just kept asking questions. She came up with good ideas.

"Good thinking, Tracy. Please proceed. I'll follow up with you next week."

And I did.

I was pleased with our progress in the Paint shop, but every step forward revealed how much further we had to go. And how little time we had.

A Night in Astoria

Things were getting better at the plant, but I still had trouble in my personal life, mainly due to my ex-wife. Sophie's seventh birthday was coming up. We had planned a birthday party. Would she give me the girls?

My lawyer, Deb Lucas had called me and said, "Don't worry, my love. The girls will be there."

Deb always calls me "my love." She is a good lawyer and a friend. She has a smoky contralto and moonlights as a jazz singer. Deb said she had alerted the "other side" about the birthday party and was working on our court application. I wanted more time with my children and fewer hassles.

"She must be quite a specimen," said Sarah. She meant my ex.

"I wish she was in formaldehyde."

"You have to find a way to get along with her, Tom."

"I'm trying."

Sarah was terrific. I was going to introduce her to my girls this weekend. I was nervous about it. Like all kids, Sophie and Helen wanted Mommy and Daddy to live together. Meeting Sarah would cause all sorts of questions to surface. "Do you still love us?" "Will you still be our daddy?" "Will she be our mommy?" "Will we still spend time with you?"

We had a long daddy-daughters chat.

"Mommy and Daddy love you more than anything in the whole wide world," I told them. "We got married because we *really* wanted to have you. But we didn't get along and we're happier living apart."

"Daddy has a new friend," I continued. "Her name is Sarah, and she is very nice. She teaches second grade."

"Mommy lives alone," said Helen.

"Mommy likes to live alone, sweetheart. That's how some people are."

"Is she your girlfriend?" asked Sophie.

"Yes she is, Sophie."

"Is she going to be our mommy?" asked Helen.

"No, Helen, nobody will ever replace your mommy," I stressed.

"Will we still spend time with you?"

"Of course you will. As a matter of fact, I want to spend more time together."

"Do you love Sarah more than us?" asked Sophie.

"No Sophie, I love you and Helen more than anyone in the whole world."

"Well, maybe it's okay if we meet her," said Helen.

I had also invited Andy. "Sorry, Tom-san, but I am going to a Buddhist retreat in Massachusetts. May I have a rain check?"

"You got it, sensei. Enjoy the weekend."

So there we were in early Friday evening traffic going to the Upper East Side to pick up the girls. Then it was to

Astoria for dinner. Sarah could tell I was nervous. Why were the simplest things so hard?

I parked out front, said "Hi" to the doorman and walked into the elegant marble foyer. Nice old Manhattan building. I took the elevator up. I knocked on the door, expecting the worst.

I heard voices. The door opened . . . two grinning moppets.

"Hi, Daddy!"

"Hi, girls! Who is ready for a great weekend?"

"We are, Dad!"

"Well, let's go then," I told them.

"I expect them back on Sunday at six-thirty," said my ex-wife.

To hear is to obey.

"And I don't want your parents giving them any chocolate."

You speak and it shall be so.

"Have a nice weekend, Teal."

Sarah was waiting for us in the foyer. She knelt down and said, "Hi, I'm Sarah. I've heard so much about you." The girls took to her immediately and insisted that she sit in the back seat between them.

We took the 59th Street bridge across the East River into Queens. I made a left at 31st Street and we were in Astoria, my home turf. Every street corner told a story. I slowed down and pointed out landmarks.

"Hey girls, there's St. Irene's, where you were baptized!"

"We know, Dad."

"There's Christos Billiards, where the Greeks chased Daddy and Uncle Harry with pool cues."

"Christos?" asked Sarah. "They named a pool room after Christ?"

"Christos Papoulakis. It's a common Greek name. Chris is very religious."

"Why did they chase you with pool cues?"

"Well, we threw pails of water into the fresh air fans, which soaked all the patrons. We were kids."

"Of course," she said.

"There's the school yard where we used to play stick ball, girls. And if you make a left here at 24th Street, you'll get to Astoria Park where we used to have picnics by the water, looking out over Manhattan."

"We know, Dad."

Street signs and store windows were now in English and Greek; here and there the Stars and Stripes hung next to the blue and white of Greece. There was the Varsity Cinema where I got my first kiss. Watching an Al Pacino flick with Jenny Lazaridis, bless her.

There was the old variety store Stavros Stavridis used to run. The memories ... Harry and I filling little paper bags with caramels, rockets and sweet tarts ... kindly Stavros, God rest his soul, smiling behind bifocals. Around the corner was Blessed Heart, Dino's school, where we played floor hockey in the Parish Hall.

"And here at the corner of 31st and Ditmars is ..."

"The Humpty Dumpty!" the girls sang out.

We parked out front and I pointed out the GOO F sign, which made everybody laugh. It was a warm spring night, and Dad had set up a little outdoor patio. It was busy for early Friday evening.

Uncle Louie was working the bar. "Tommy my boy!" he shouted. He has a big stomach and a shiny bullet head.

"Uncle Louie!" the girls hollered, running up to him.

"Ti kanete, my little angels? You should speak Greek to them," he told me sotto voce.

He turned to Sarah. "And who would this lovely young woman be?"

Sarah introduced herself. "What a character," she whispered.

"Uncle Louie, can you do Curly?" the children pleaded.

Louie nyuked it up; the girls howled with laughter. "I'm working on Shemp," he declared.

"At our house it was Plato, Aristotle and the Three Stooges," I told Sarah.

Hearing the commotion, my mom and dad peeked out through the serving window. Dad came out of the kitchen first. "MY GOODNESS, MY GOODNESS, MY GOODNESS!"

The girls ran to him. He kissed them, then me. "How are you, my boy?"

"I'm well, Dad. How are you, Mama?"

She embraced me. "Couldn't be better, Tommy. Aren't you going to introduce us?"

We did the introductions, and Dad directed us to a booth. "You must be starving. The lamb is excellent tonight."

The kids ordered cheeseburgers. Sarah ordered roast leg of lamb, and I went with the lamb and spinach fricassee. Mama brought out a bottle of Greek white and a tray of appetizers. "You must try my mezedes."

Mom and Dad sat and chatted with us as we ate. "We've already eaten," they said.

Sarah was taking it all in. Spin-around stools and the long front counter, blue-clothed tables and orange vinyl booths. Corfu travel posters, corny celebrity photos; the regulars reading the paper or kibitzing with staff; Uncle Louie pouring beer from gleaming spouts. Waiters picking up their orders at the serving window. Someone lit up a cigarette. Nobody bothered him.

"You have a wonderful restaurant," said Sarah.

"Thank you, my dear," Mama replied. "Every day I pray to St. Spyridon for my Tommy. He's the patron saint of Corfu, where we came from."

"That's right," Dad put in. "Our family comes from a little village called Giapades, in the Ropa valley. About twenty minutes from Corfu Town, the prettiest town in all of Greece! You know, we still have property there, which my cousin Manolis looks after. We have olive trees, apple, pear and cherry trees. We have a beautiful orchard by a stream. In the spring it's full of fish."

"It sounds wonderful," said Sarah.

Maybe I'll take you there, I thought.

"It's God's country," added Mama, with a dreamy look. "Don't get me wrong, we love America, but Corfu is something else."

Sunlight poured in orange, pink and violet. Sarah squeezed my hand. And the next day Sophie had her best birthday ever.

Visual Management

Spring was here, and with the change in weather we got more dirt in the Paint shop. It was a ventilation system problem, and Freddie had assigned his best engineer. But it was a long-term fix. In the interim, we still had to ship 60 good cars per hour to Assembly.

Spot repair was the key to maintaining our throughput. We have six repair bays, each with a cycle time of 30 minutes. Theoretically, we could salvage 12 units per hour, or 20 percent of our throughput. We wouldn't need to run overtime. In effect, spot repair had become our constraint in Paint shop. So Andy and I went over to Paint shop to investigate.

It was a cloudy afternoon. The barometric pressure had been bouncing around the past few days, which always affected our paint quality. We took the shortcut near the paint sludge pit and went in a side door. We pulled white Tyvek suits over our clothes, put on hairnets and went into the shop.

Spot repair was over by final line. We went over to see the money board, which, I was happy to see, was visible and current. From there we watched the conveyor to spot repair filling up with cars.

"What is current condition at spot repair?" Andy asked me.

"We have units in four of six repair bays and eighteen more coming. There are two repairmen."

"What is our delivery status?"

I looked over the money board. "It doesn't look good. It's close to shift end, and we're fifty-two units below target. We'll start the next shift in the hole. If not for the automatic storage and retrieval building, assembly would be idle."

Andy nodded. "Eighteen units on conveyor to spot repair—is this normal or abnormal, Tom-san?"

"Well, it's abnormal. We usually have five or six."

"Two repairmen at spot repair—is that normal or abnormal?"

"That's normal, sensei."

"So, we have a major abnormality at our constraint; delivery target at risk, but we have only two repairmen," Andy summed up.

I was embarrassed. What a mess. We didn't have a standard or any visual management. I could tell we were in trouble, but could anyone else? Why weren't there more repairmen at spot repair? Freddie was out of the shop. But shouldn't it happen automatically?

The thoughts kept coming. Why was our cycle time so long? Why did we use large baking lights for small repairs? Couldn't we buy small heaters? Why were there only six repair holes?

"Sensei, we need visual management," I said.

I turned to the visual management triangle in my journal.

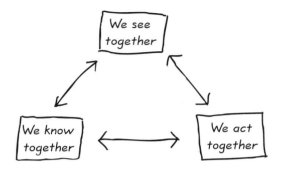

Then I had an epiphany.

"Sensei, I've got it! We need to paint the spot repair conveyor as follows:

- Zero to five units: green,
- Six to ten: yellow, and
- Ten or more: red.

When there's an abnormality everyone will know. 'Hey, we need more repair people at spot repair.'"

"Good! But Freddie-san is not here. How to ensure countermeasure is automatic?"

At Taylor Motors, only the manager can move people around. Could we delegate such decisions to supervisors?

"Sensei, our plant needs to work like a vast immune system! We need empowered intelligence at every point, which means clear visible standards, better training and decision-making power."

Andy laughed. "Too much bourbon last night! Your image is powerful, but we are not ready. We must take small steps. Today we must focus on spot repair. Let's go."

On our way to spot repair, we passed the inspection deck. Greetings rang out. "Yo, Tommy! Yo, sensei!"

"What's happening at spot repair?" I asked Yvonne, the inspection deck team leader.

"They're really backed up," she said. "We've been having spits and dirt all day. I *told* them we needed more repairmen."

My brilliant ideas were just common knowledge.

When we got to spot repair, Clayton, the supervisor, told me we were way behind. "I don't know how we're going to catch up," he said.

"Can anyone else do repair work?"

"Bernie up in prime scuff and Mo in enamel. They're pretty good."

"Let's get them down here."

Clay got on the radio. "Bernie and Mo are coming down."

"Thanks, Clay. Any way we can shorten our cycle time?"

"Get us those portable bake units I saw in Kansas City. They are fine. We could cut ten minutes off a repair job."

"Go ahead and order them."

"We've been asking for two years, Tom. But Freddie says no new equipment."

Again, I felt embarrassed. That was my doing. "I'll talk to him, Clay."

Spot repair is a high-skill job. You have to dig out the defect, fill and seal the hole. I looked around for visual aids, standardized work charts—nothing. How would a new repairman know what to do?

We threw new team members into deep water and kept those that survived. Most of our repair people are near retirement. Did we have a succession plan? Had we ever helped Clayton with training in problem solving or visual management? I had to talk to Andy about human resources.

Andy was chatting with Shafiq, one of the repairmen. "What colors do you use? What tools and jigs do you use? Do you ever lose anything?"

"I lose my jigs all the time," Shafiq replied. "And my paint cans, too. I've told them we need tool boards but nobody listens."

"I like that idea, Shafiq," I put in. "Would you design one?"

"I'd be happy to, Tom."

"Thank you for making problem visible," said Andy. "Now we must work together to fix."

We walked back to the money board. It told quite a story. The supervisors had just posted the last hour's results. Sure enough, we were in trouble. Our FTT was only 58 percent for the day. Each zone would have to run overtime to meet our delivery target of 480 units. But there was much more.

Zone A was struggling with poor metal quality—Sylvain shipping garbage again. They were swamped in the metal repair booth. All that sanding and grinding was generating dirt. And that dirt was killing Zone D—which is why spot repair was so busy. It was a vicious cycle. The only way to stop it was to improve metal quality coming out of the Body shop.

Paint Shop Money Board								
Date: 5/14		Shift: Days				Superintendent: T. West		
		Zone A		Zone B		Zone C		Zone D	
Hour	Production plan (hr/cum)	Actual production (hr/cum)	Offline repairs	Actual production (hr/cum)	Offline repairs	Actual production (hr/cum)	Offline repairs	Actual production (hr/cum)	Offline repairs
1	60/60	50/50	5	55/60	3	50/60	9	48/48	11
2	60/120	55/105	7	50/105	7	53/103	6	52/100	7
3	60/180	49/154	8	55/160	3	57/160	1	53/153	6
4	60/240	50/204	7	58/218	1	55/215	4	56/209	4
5	60/300	44/248	13	57/275	2	51/266	8	50/259	9
6	60/360	50/298	3	50/325	8	51/317	7	47/306	12
7	60/420	39/337	18	55/380	4	56/373	3	50/356	8
8	60/480	53/390	5	56/436	2	50/423	9	45/401	13
9									
10									
Total	480	390	66	436	30	423	47	401	70
Top three problems		Metal quality– dents, dings, creases, weld spatter		Primer coverage thin in trunk area		Enamel coverage thin on rocker panel Overspray– wheel wells		Dirt & spits on roof Mars– left fender	

First time through (480-66-30-47-70)/480 = 58%

Would I ever get a better lesson in visual management?
I was about to get another lesson.

"Tom-san, what did you see in spot repair?" Andy
asked.

"I saw stuff all over the work tables and the floor. Paint
cans, jigs, gloves, rags . . . it was hard to say what belonged."

"Current cycle time is thirty minutes. How much is
waste?"

"You've taught me all repair work is waste. Therefore, one-hundred percent of spot repair is waste."

Andy nodded. "In longer term, we must reduce the need for spot repair. But today we need it. So, how much of the current process is waste?"

"The only valuable activities are digging, filling and baking. Everything else is waste."

"How can we reduce waste, Tom-san?"

"Making a shadow board for our tools would be a good start," I told him. "Shafiq will do that. It'll tell us what should be there and what's actually there. But we need to apply the 5S system to the entire area."

"Before we discuss 5S, I will give you some homework. What is the *ideal* cycle time for spot repair?"

"I'll have to do a time study."

Andy nodded. "Please review with Freddie-san. Now please explain, what is 5S?"

I repeated what I had learned in Joe Grace's lunch and learn. "Five S is a system of workplace organization and standardization. S1 stands for sort out what you don't need. S2 means set in order. S3 stands for shine or clean. S4 means standardize and S5 means sustain."

"How can we apply 5S in spot repair?"

"Sensei, I don't really understand five S. I'm just repeating what I heard."

Andy walked to the nearby white board and drew a large circle. "We have much stuff on spot repair deck."

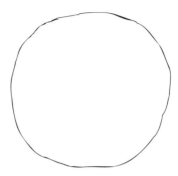

"S1: Sort out what you don't need. We must decide what is needed and what is *not* needed."

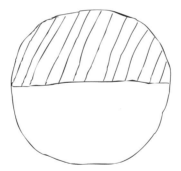

"S2: Set in order. We must organize what is left."

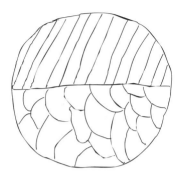

"Now we must ask, 'Where is it, what is it and how many?' We must organize along X, Y and Z axes."

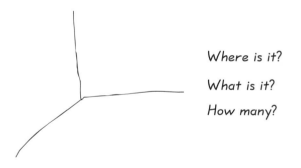

Where is it?

What is it?

How many?

"We must use colors and pictures to make it easy to understand," Andy continued.

I absorbed this the way a child absorbs the alphabet.

"Now, we have some space, some order. We can shine the workplace—S3. We must decide who, what, when and how to clean and what support team members will need. We must provide tape, paint and cleaning materials."

"We have to confirm that with the union," I put in. "They can be sticky about lines of demarcation."

"Of course, we must develop shared understanding with union. Some people believe Japanese unions and labor laws are not so difficult. Not true. In Japan we have very strong unions and labor laws. At Toyota in the 1950s we had much labor strife. Shoiichiro Toyoda had to resign as president!

"But we learned from our mistakes, and we worked hard to develop trust with a shared understanding. We made a commitment to job security. But we said, 'Please, help us to improve. Please do the work that needs to be done.' Taylor Motors must develop same understanding.

"Anyhow," he continued, "After S3 we have a clean, organized workplace. But soon, it will deteriorate. So we need S4—standardize. What does standardize mean, Tom-san?"

I looked over at spot repair. "S4 means standardizing S1, S2 and S3. S1 standards should help us decide what to keep. S2 standards should address colors, signage, tool boards and equipment footprints. S3 standards should tell us who, when, where and how to clean. S3 also means visual aids for critical SQDC points." I was on a roll.

"Good, Tom-san! What is S5—sustain?"

"Sustain means doing things that will maintain a good condition."

"Just maintain?"

"Maintain and improve," I replied. "Sustain means 5S walks and team boards. Sustain means ownership, the feeling that this is *our* workplace. It also means training and problem solving."

Andy nodded. "Now please explain how to apply five S to spot repair."

"First we clear out excess stuff. Then we apply visual order through tool and jig boards and visual aids for quality."

"How do we organize materials?" Andy was relentless.

"We need home positions."

"How do we prevent build-up?"

I had a brainwave and drew it on the whiteboard. "How about making little rings for the paint cans to sit in? If we had too many, we'd know at a glance."

Andy grinned. "Much artwork today."

Next day I asked Joe Grace to get money board pilots going in all departments. I asked Jeff and Freddie to standardize our team, department and plant boards. I had seen the power of visual management. I wanted everyone to see, know and act together.

But I had also seen just how vulnerable we were. An abnormality in one area could quickly spread throughout the plant. The Body shop was becoming our plant's constraint, and I knew a showdown was inevitable.

Driving home that night, I noticed the parking lot gate. It hadn't been damaged in over a month.

Maybe there was hope.

The River and the Rocks

"Overproduction is the worst form of waste. I finally understand that, sensei." Andy, Joe and I were having sushi after a long day. I had given Joe all my notes on visual management and 5S. He had turned them into a good lunch and learn. He had also launched money board pilots in all shops.

It was a warm night, and we were eating alfresco. We started with unagi and frosty Sapporos.

"When you make stuff nobody ordered, you waste labor and materials," I went on. "You need extra space, which you have to rent, heat and secure. You need more forklifts and drivers. It takes longer to find stuff amid the piles of inventory. Overproduction degrades quality because it's harder to find defects. It cuts people off from one another. You can't see over all the storage racks."

Andy nodded. "Why do we overproduce at New Jersey Motor Manufacturing? Please do five-why analysis." Andy had taught us this simple problem-solving tool. The key was to think simply, like a child, and not to jump to conclusions. I found it difficult.

Joe piped up. "First why: Why do workers overproduce? Because the manager tells them to. Second why: Why do managers tell them to overproduce? Because they think they'll need extra in case of quality problems or machine breakdowns."

"We also overproduce to make our efficiency numbers look better," I said. "Overproduction soaks up overhead. It keeps Jed Morgan off our backs."

Then it hit me.

"Standard cost accounting was developed to support traditional mass production!" I continued. "It assumes you make money by running flat out to lower unit costs. But it doesn't measure the cost of overproduction or bad quality or late deliveries."

Joe took it further. "So financial control in our system means checking the mountain of inventory as it moves through the plant. We generate thousands of accounting transactions. We track direct and indirect cost, fixed and variable cost. We create labor and machine utilization 'standards.' Does it help us improve the business?"

Andy nodded. "Good analysis. Please continue."

"Well, now we've got two branches." I drew it out on a napkin.

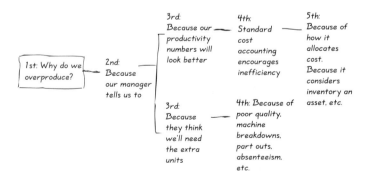

"You and your napkins," Andy commented.

"You can take the boy out of the diner..." I said. "Seems to me, we should focus on the second branch, because that's the one we control."

Andy agreed. "I am discussing accounting issues with Rachel-san."

"Therefore," I continued, "the root cause of overproduction is poor quality, machine breakdowns, part-outs and so on. We have to flood our system with inventory to keep running. The assembly storage and retrieval building is a good example. I remember you frowning when you first saw it."

"Please don't misunderstand, Tom-san. Without ASRB, we cannot meet our delivery target. Sometimes we need to increase inventory—but only until we stabilize. Then we must challenge ourselves to *reduce* it.

"Inventory hides problems the way a river hides rocks."

He drew it out for us in his journal.

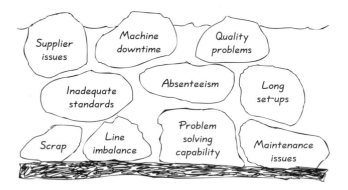

"To make the rocks *visible* we must lower the water level."

I mulled it over. Inventory concealed problems. To improve we had to reduce it. And the corollary: A factory's capability is inversely proportional to its inventory level. World-class plants run lean. Second-rate plants swim in inventory.

The main course arrived—sushi and tempura. I tried a piece of tuna. Joe sampled the tempura. "Sensei," he asked, "how big is the ASRB at a typical Toyota plant?"

"There is no ASRB at Toyota plants," Andy replied. "The buffer between the Paint and Assembly departments is normally twenty to thirty units."

Joe and I were silent. We had 600 units in the ASRB. Were we that far behind Toyota?

"Do not feel bad. The most important thing is to improve every day. When I was a young engineer at Takaoka plant, we had the same problems. Inventory is like drug addiction. We must reduce dependence slowly."

So that's why team member involvement is vital, I thought. Without it, how could we find, let alone fix, all the hidden problems? But we had to give workers something back. Something they value. Like job security; like respect. TPS was coming together for me. Everything was connected to everything else. No wonder it had taken Taiichi Ohno and Eiji Toyoda 30 years to drive it through Toyota.

I took a pull on my Sapporo. "Sensei, what was Taiichi Ohno like?"

"Tough."

"How about Eiji Toyoda?" Joe put in.

"Also tough! There was much opposition to TPS in the early years. Ohno-san was difficult, demanding. He was severe with team members, suppliers and deshi too. Ohno-san made many enemies, but Toyoda-san supported him."

I was impressed. "You were Taiichi Ohno's deshi?"

"Yes, I spent five years with Ohno-san. He was a difficult sensei, but very generous, very kind to me."

I pictured him as a young engineer at Takaoka, working with the obnoxious genius who was turning the world upside down. How lucky we've been, I thought.

He looked at us. "So, what is the next step?"

I took a deep breath. "We need to start lowering the water level."

"We need to make our problems visible," Joe added.

"Why not set up minimum and maximum inventory levels between departments?" he continued. "If the Paint shop were to go down, then the Body shop would stop producing when it hit its maximum. The accordion of inventory would start to contract. We could install limit switches to conveyors to stop production when inventory reached the maximum. Later we could apply min/max levels *within* departments and at our repair bays. Hitting trigger points would trigger action. We would need visual management. We've already started at spot repair."

"I like it, Joe," I said. "Our working capital and lead time would drop sharply. We'd have more space. We'd need fewer parts and fewer forklift trucks to deliver them. Production departments would feel connected. But there are big obstacles.

"We'd have to fix the abnormalities in each of the 4 Ms—man and woman, method, machine and material. Absenteeism, ergonomics, process capability, preventative maintenance ... my head hurts just thinking about it."

I remembered Fukuda's parable. Grumblers like Sylvain would seize upon the problems as proof that we didn't know what we were doing. I knew he was feeding Jed Morgan information. To hell with them, I thought. Ohno and Toyoda have shown us the way, paddling in the dark, against the current. We can do it, too. We *will* do it.

"Saito-san, your senseis were very tough."

"Yes," he said. "And we are also tough."

I now understood why we needed so much inventory. Each of the 4 Ms—man and woman, method, machine and material—was unstable. Inventory covered up our problems. I knew which one I had to fix next.

People Make the Difference

It was a soft summer night, and I couldn't sleep. We were improving across the board, but not as quickly as I wanted. I had found one of our biggest obstacles—the way we managed our people. I was forming a plan.

We ignored human resources at our plant. HR handled dull stuff like grievances and worker's comp. When our last HR manager retired, we didn't replace her. But with Andy's help, I had conceived a different role.

People were at the heart of TPS. Andy said that HR was the "pacemaker department" for:

- Safety.
- Recruitment.
- Training and development.
- Involvement.
- Culture.

This meant HR needed to develop deep knowledge, clear simple standards and robust processes. Then they had to teach us and practice PDCA. Could our HR team handle it?

I didn't think so. I needed a champion.

Could Antonio do it? He knew the Toyota system. He was transforming the Stamping department. His team was becoming self-sufficient, so maybe he could moonlight. But could I really put a Stamping manager into human resources?

I fell asleep with that question rattling around in my brain. The following morning I ran the idea by Joe Grace. "It's radical," he said. "I like it." Andy's support clinched it.

Antonio laughed when I asked if he'd do it. "Are you kidding? I would love to."

"You'll be working longer hours."

"I don't mind, Tom. Not long ago I was ready to leave Taylor Motors. But now I love my work. We are creating something out of chaos."

"Antonio, I'd like to ask you an unrelated question. Please answer frankly. What are we going to do about Sylvain?"

"John has energy and intelligence. But his mind is closed."

"The Body shop has become our constraint," I told him.

"Everyone knows it."

"We're going there next. Any advice?"

"John is hurting," he said. "He didn't think our plan would work. But now everybody is improving except him. Be careful."

"Thanks. Now let's talk about human resources."

I described my epiphany in the Paint shop: the plant as a vast immune system, engaged team members identifying and correcting abnormalities at each point based on clear visible standards and their own understanding, gained through job rotation and ownership.

Antonio liked it. "How do we make it real?" I asked. We spent the next few hours brainstorming. Here is the first draft of our tree diagram, which Antonio would turn into an A3 strategy.

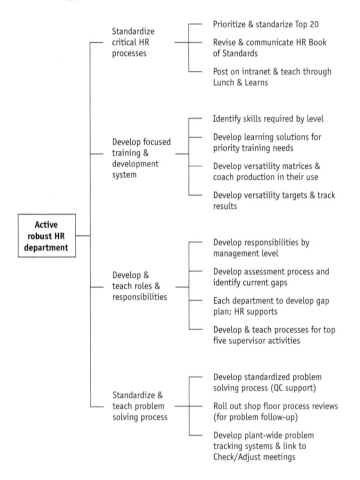

I presented our tree diagram to Joe and Andy over a cafeteria lunch.

"HR has to become process driven. This is the first branch of our tree. For example, our recruitment process has to be one-hundred percent capable. If we need a hundred good people, we have to hire a hundred good people. That means defining 'good.' Antonio and I believe that 'good' means:

- Honest,
- Trustworthy,
- Able to follow standardized work,
- Solves problems and
- Likes working in a team.

"We've made bad hiring decisions over the years," I continued, "people who didn't like manufacturing work or who couldn't work in a team. Many of our people are retiring in the next few years. If we survive—knock on wood—we'll need good people to replace them."

I paused. Andy had his eyes closed. Joe was chewing on a slice of pizza. "I'm listening," he said.

"Me too," said Andy.

I took a bite of my cheeseburger, had a sip of water and went on.

"Training and development is weak. This is the second branch of our tree. We need to define required skills by position. We ask supervisors to practice PDCA and drive problem solving. But do they have the needed skills? And do we have learning solutions to fill any gaps?

"We also need to pilot job rotation. It keeps the mind and body fresh. Toyota team members rotate every two hours. No wonder they're happier. No wonder there are fewer injuries."

Andy had opened his eyes and was eating a butter tart. Joe was wolfing down a piece of apple pie.

I sampled a carrot stick and continued. "We also have to standardize management activities. This is the third branch of our tree. Freddie has scored with pre- and post-shift meetings. Why not develop and teach standards for:

- 5S walks,
- Quality checks,
- Safety and
- Problem solving?

"Management needs a cadence, a rhythm. Standards *support* creativity. As a musician I know this instinctively. The sheet music doesn't constrain the players; it liberates them.

"Finally, we have to get better at problem solving. This is the fourth branch of our tree. We need to link problem solving to plant goals through policy management. We need to make progress visible through a simple, shared database."

Joe went up to the serving area and came back with coffee and toothpicks.

"Well, what do you think of our HR strategy?" I asked them.

"Go for it," they answered.

Over the summer Antonio made major improvements in our HR system. And we were ready to tackle an even bigger obstacle.

"No Problem" is a Problem

Andy, Jeff Turner and I were eating "al desko" in an Assembly shop team room. Hawaiian pizza (al dente) and diet Coke (sprizzicato). Mama would have been horrified. I had just delivered my PDCA lunch and learn for Jeff's supervisors. It had gone well—plenty of questions. The supervisors were heading back to the line; we were having the leftovers.

It was early September, and we had been making steady progress for six months. I was proud of Jeff, who had embraced TPS and was driving it in Assembly, our money shop. He and Freddie had also done a fine job teaching standardization. More and more problems were becoming visible. Now we had to do something about them.

"Sensei, what do you think of Six Sigma?" I asked.

We had launched Six Sigma, a sophisticated problem-solving system, a few years back. The business press was full of success stories. But we had little to show for it.

Andy had made a face. "What is the biggest problem in factory, Tom-san?"

"Process instability."

"How can we stabilize processes?"

"Jeff, do you want to answer this one?"

"We need simple visible standards for the four M's," he said. "We need to make problems visible, so we can solve them."

"What kind of problems are we seeing?" Andy asked.

"Basic problems, like chips and scratches, water leaks, wrong parts or missing parts," Jeff answered.

"So what kind of problem-solving method do we need?"

"I get it sensei," I said. "We need to walk before we can run."

Andy nodded. "Who is the most important person for problem solving?"

I mulled it over. "I think the supervisor is most important."

"Correct! And so, we need a problem-solving process the supervisor can use," Andy concluded.

He told us that, as a young engineer, he too had been in thrall of advanced statistical methods like Six Sigma. But he had learned that 90 percent of problems could be solved with a simple method that he called "practical problem solving." Advanced statistical methods like Six Sigma could handle the rest.

Andy went to the whiteboard and drew it out.

Practical Problem Solving

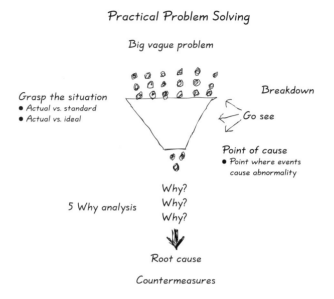

"This image shows the thinking way," he explained. "Now I will show you the process."

Andy continued to draw on the whiteboard (see pages 126–127). We heard the whine of the conveyor. The line was starting up. We weren't going anywhere. Time seemed to dissolve as he took us through each step. It was complicated on the surface but simple and elegant in principle. We absorbed it like children watching a juggler.

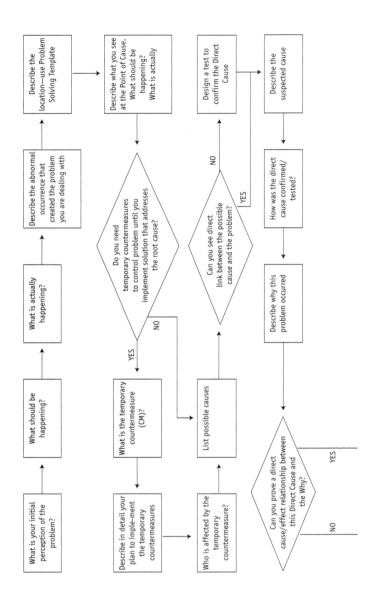

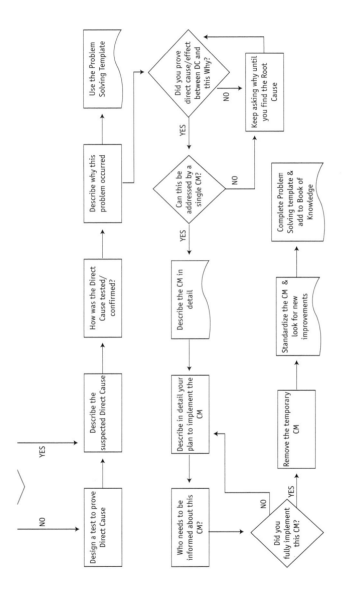

"Jeff, do you think we can build a problem-solving system around this process?"

"Absolutely," he replied.

"Good. We'll need a problem-solving template, training and a shared database. I want everyone to know what problems are open and who needs help. I know it's a big job. Make a plan and tell me what help you need."

Over the next week, I focused my attention on the Body shop. Sylvain continued to be a jerk. He shipped garbage but wouldn't own up to it. He was sullen and argumentative. He didn't like it when Freddie and the other senior managers challenged him. But he was still good at manipulating the accounting numbers.

But the fact was, the Body shop had become our constraint. Quality was poor, as was delivery. Robots, presses and transfers kept breaking down. Sylvain was running overtime most weekdays and on weekends. The yard was full of his scrap.

We were missing 100 out of 2,700 welds on the hard top of the Desperado. So the body fit was lousy, which meant water leaks and wind noise. Surface quality also stunk. Freddie put an extra man in metal repair to fix all the dents and dings, but this just generated dust, which meant more units in spot repair—a vicious cycle.

I thought I knew what was happening but wanted to confirm my thinking with Andy. We met in the Assembly shop, in the water test area. Shiny Desperados went past us and into the booth while we chatted.

"Sensei, overall equipment effectiveness (OEE) is the critical metric in the Body shop.

OEE = Availability × Efficiency × Quality Rate

"Availability is the percent uptime; efficiency measures effectiveness of machines while they're running; the quality rate reflects the amount of scrap."

Andy nodded.

"We measure OEE at the bottleneck," I continued. "In Body, the bottleneck is Body buck, where the parts come together to make the body. The welding robots there are prone to breakdowns.

"Sylvain has been reporting an OEE of eighty percent. But I found we were only measuring uptime. Our actual OEE is closer to fifty percent, which makes Body the plant constraint. We won't get better until the Body shop gets better."

"You are grasping the situation," Andy remarked.

Next day I called Bill Barrett. "The Body shop is our constraint, Bill. I'm thinking of putting Joe Grace in there to help Sylvain. What do you think?"

Dean Formica had given me the idea during our last chat. If I couldn't fire Sylvain, maybe I could go around him.

"I'm okay with it, Tommy," Bill replied. "But please keep a cool head and ask Joe to do the same. Jed Morgan is turning up the heat. Let's not give him any more ammo."

"Oh, for crying out loud!" I said. "We're hitting our delivery targets every day. We're making the highest quality Desperado ever. We've freed up millions of dollars through scrap and inventory reduction. What else does Morgan want?"

"You're doing a great job," Bill agreed. "I'm riding shot gun. But please handle Sylvain with finesse."

"Bill, are you afraid of Jed Morgan?"

"Yes I am, Tom. But that doesn't mean I'm going to back down."

"Is Rachel Armstrong afraid of him?"

He laughed. "Rachel isn't afraid of anything."

After talking with Bill, I went straight to Sylvain's office on the other side of the plant. I had tried hard to motivate Sylvain. But his mental models were entirely different.

Sylvain wasn't in his office. Sure enough, I found him in the Body control room monitoring a breakdown via computer. We exchanged pleasantries.

"John," I said. "I'd like you to set up a review meeting, ASAP. Please invite your management team. Let's have it between shifts so everyone can attend. I'd like you to report your current condition, and especially the hot spots and what you're doing about them. After your presentation, Mr. Saito will describe Toyota's approach to maintenance. One more thing, the next few months Joe Grace will be working with you in Body."

Sylvain didn't look happy.

Five days later, Andy, Joe and I were in the Body shop team room. Everybody was there: engineers, production and maintenance supervisors and specialists. Sylvain and Gio

Bellini, his young engineering manager, had the Virtual Manufacturer software up on the screen. They were describing Little's law, a mathematical model that's supposed to help you exploit your constraint.

"We need to find heuristic solutions," Gio said, glancing nervously at Sylvain.

Andy was holding a cool pop can to his forehead. I wished I had one, too. The production supervisors got up next. It was a joke. They didn't know what was happening in their zones. Their pagers and radios kept going off. "Please turn them off," I said. The place reeked of tension.

When it was finally over, Andy turned to Sylvain. "Thank you, John-san for good presentation. Now please tell us, what are the Body shop's problems?"

"We don't have any problems," Sylvain replied. "Just a few minor setbacks lately."

Andy repeated the question.

"I just told you we don't have any problems!"

Andy looked at Sylvain. "No problem is a problem."

Sylvain glared back. "What does that mean?"

"No problem, no need for manager."

Gio and the supervisors looked about anxiously. Sylvain was red-faced. The room had suddenly become very quiet.

Developing Early Warning Systems

On the other side of the wall, we could hear the clang-rattle-shush of production. But on this side, nobody was saying anything. Andy wasn't trying to insult Sylvain. He was simply stating what was obvious to him. Without problems, a manager would have nothing to do. Problems were to be welcomed, not feared. "No problem" meant we weren't looking hard enough.

"We should say 'thank you' to problems," Andy continued. "Maybe we don't understand what a problem is. Who can explain?"

Nervous glances, foot-tapping, neck-scratching. Joe Grace was taking it all in, like a black Buddha.

Finally, someone hollered, "A problem is when something is not going the way it should!"

"Yeah, like when a robot misses a weld," another chimed in.

"Or faults out because the skid is bent," said a third.

"Or when we get sealer all over the car!"

"Or when the hayrack gets stuck!"

The ice was broken. Andy smiled. "Good! A problem means something is not right; something is *out of standard*. Now who can explain what standard is?"

Gio piped up. "A standard is what should be happening."

"Yes, Gio-san! And what is a problem?"

"A problem is the difference between what *should* be happening and what is *actually* happening!" The kid had been listening.

"Very good!" Andy drew it out on the white board.

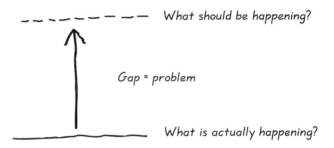

"If we have no standard, we do not have a problem," Andy continued. "We have a *concern*—a vague idea that something is wrong. So the first step is to make a good standard."

The Body shop team was not used to simplicity. Andy drew on the whiteboard some more. "Now we will talk about Total Productive Maintenance, the Toyota system. There are four stages of TPM." (See next page.)

"With respect, John-san, we are at the most basic stage. We must stabilize equipment first. Where are the constraints? Any of the four M's can be a constraint.

"How can we protect our constraints? We can use buffers or we can back them up manually. Once our constraints are protected, we can solve problems, we can focus maintenance activities. How to focus our activities?"

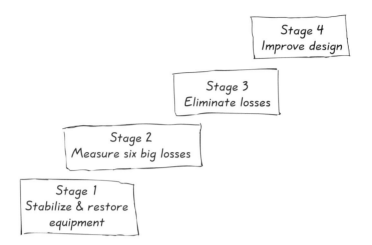

Andy let the question sink in. Sylvain's face was a clenched fist.

"Imagine the Body shop is like hospital," Andy continued. "Machines are patients; maintenance and engineering are doctors. Some are general practitioners; others are specialists—electrical, hydraulics, pneumatics and so on. What type of medicine do we need to practice in Body shop?"

"Gerontology!" someone sang out, which got a big laugh.

"Correct!" said Andy. "We need a daily check and adjust for elderly patients. We also need to make problems visible. How can we do this?"

Again, the furtive glances at Sylvain. I repeated Andy's question. "How can we make problems more visible?"

A pregnant silence. We had reached a tipping point.

"Well, we could make a problem status board and review it every day," Gio said.

"Okay," I put in. "But how do we create ownership?"

"There should be a case manager, like at a hospital," said Rebecca Johnson, a young mechanical engineer from Texas. "The case manager brings in specialists as required."

"We could track progress like they do in a hospital," Gio added.

"Please show us," I told him.

Gio went to the whiteboard. "Let's call it Machine Symptom Investigation. We don't want to wait for problems. We want an *early* warning." He drew out a check sheet and a tracking board (see next page).

"We can put case details on the back of the symptom investigation form," Gio went on. "Like, what specialist you're bringing in, and what happened."

He was a bright kid. The group mulled it over. I liked where it was going.

"Gio, we'll have both temporary and permanent countermeasures," Rebecca put in. "So we need two columns."

"Good point, Becky," I said. "But how are we going to record status?"

"How about red, yellow and green?" Gio suggested.

"We need to be more concrete," said Becky. "I saw something at our Kansas City plant. They called it the pie system." She drew it for us.

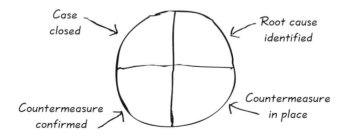

Machine Symptom Investigation		
A. Machine:	Zone:	
Supervisor:	Area:	
Date:	Process:	

Machine drawing/ description	**B.** Symptom(s) description:	

C. Symptom(s) caused by:		

D. Countermeasures	Date	Responsibility

Supervisor	Eng. Mgr.	Maint. Mgr.

Machine Symptom Investigation Tracking Board						
Machine	Zone	Problem	Case Mgr.	Counter-measure	Status	Next Steps

"Any comments?" I asked. There was a buzz of agreement.

"We have the makings of a system," I summed up. "But we have to figure out the details. Like, who decides what gets on the board? What happens if a problem lags? How do we assign case managers? Who drives the check and adjust meeting? I nominate Gio and Rebecca as joint owners of the process. John, you okay with that?"

Sylvain was beyond caring. He managed a grunt.

"Gio and Rebecca will confirm process details with John and will drive the meetings. We also need targets for overall equipment effectiveness, mean time to repair and mean time between failure.

"John, please put together a Body shop money board ASAP. Our current condition should be visible to everyone. I also want quick action on weld effectiveness. What's the root cause? What's the countermeasure? Please report back to me. Mr. Saito, any words of wisdom?"

"We made progress today," Andy summed up. "But we are a long way from stabilizing Body shop. Please implement the symptom investigation process. John-san, please practice and teach PDCA. Thank you very much."

"Thank you, Mr. Saito," I said.

I looked around the room. We had started a fire; I didn't want Sylvain to extinguish it.

"I have a few things to say," I told them.

I turned to Sylvain.

"I am not happy. John, I expect much more from you. We are swimming in scrap and inventory. Yet you won't even admit to having problems. Right now, I don't care about Virtual Manufacturer or about heuristic solutions. You must teach and apply our standards. That is my strong request. Do you understand?"

Sylvain looked like his head was going to explode.

I turned to the management team. "We took some baby steps today but have a long way to go. Body shop is our constraint now. Please take action. Let John know what help you need. Joe Grace will be spending a lot of time with you,"—Joe waved—"and Mr. Saito and I will be checking in regularly."

And with that I walked out the door. Andy and Joe stayed behind to work with Gio.

I was pensive walking back to the production office. I didn't like reprimanding people in public, no matter how much they deserved it. But the prize was in sight—we could save our plant—and Sylvain was our biggest obstacle. I had to take Dean's advice and go around him. Joe Grace would work with the Body shop team. He'd pull Andy in as required.

My cell phone rang. It was Rebecca Johnson.

"What can I do for you Becky?"

"I just wanted to say thanks, Tom. It's been real frustrating. John hasn't been driving anything."

"I know, Becky. But that's all going to change. I want you to work with Gio."

I asked why weld quality had deteriorated. "We've had four weld inspectors retire," she told me. "And we replaced them with unqualified people."

"Let me guess," I said. "We don't have a standard. We filled the position based on seniority."

"You got it, boss. People transfer in, thinking it's an easy job, but it isn't. Now they want their old jobs back. We'll be back in the spin cycle soon."

PDCA, standardization and human resources, I thought. We keep missing the basics. Here is a critical job, and we don't have a standard or a succession plan. I'm afraid to ask about training. We've taken baby steps, I thought. Baby steps on a thousand-mile path.

"Becky, please write up a job spec for the weld inspector position and give it to human resources. Tell Antonio we spoke."

I had been right to put Antonio in charge of HR, as well as Stamping. Administrative processes had to be as good as production processes.

I took the next couple of days off work and asked Joe Grace to mind the store. There was unfinished business in my personal life.

The Valley of Darkness

O ur day in court had arrived. Deb Lucas, my lawyer, filed a motion documenting all the garbage I had endured. We were asking for more time with the children and for a mediator to pull in whenever my ex-wife went sideways. I wanted a good working relationship with her. We had produced two beautiful children. But she had to learn to play by the rules.

I took the Lincoln Tunnel into Manhattan and made my way though midday traffic, to the county courthouse across from City Hall. Sarah met me out front. She was wearing the blue cotton dress and the silver Greek key necklace I had given her.

Sarah wrote and illustrated children's poetry. We'd have picnics in Central Park with the girls and Sarah would read. My favorite was "The Scenes of Summer":

Ah the scenes of summer!
Is any season yummer?
A field of smiling lilies
Two sheep dogs acting silly
A picnic on a hill

A tabby-cat named Bill
Honey-bees a'buzzin'
Playing leap-frog with your cousin...

Strange how much comfort I found in those words during all the bleak remembering.

Teal Orcutt. Old New Jersey money—land owners and magistrates. George Washington's army had wintered at an Orcutt farm. I remembered the early infatuation and the too-fast wedding and children. Early pride in my wife—she's a columnist, you know. Then the dawning realization that I had married the wrong woman.

Her arrogance and cruelty, always attacking and ridiculing, as if this were evidence of an independent mind. All the deep thinkers at the newspaper, people who had never manufactured anything, had never seen anything manufactured, had never hired or fired or trained a worker, had never been ripped off by a worker. People who knew nothing of the intricacies and risks of running a business—yet who believed they knew everything worth knowing.

She had barely to move a muscle—a swallow while you were speaking, a tap of her finger on the arm of the chair—to tell you that everything you were saying was wrong. It's just the environment, I'd tell myself. They're all words; that's what they do.

Not wanting to recognize that my wife was vicious—until I became the target. Clip, clip, clip—seeing how far she could push me. Torn between the abuse and the love of my daughters; my mother praying for us in St. Irene's.

Coming home that night from her staff party, Teal driving. Clip, clip, clip and I realize she's killing me by the millimeter. "Let me out at the light," I told her. Calling Joe Grace to come and pick me up, not wanting to tell my family. "I'm sorry, Tom," he said. "Stay as long as you need to."

Anguish, chaos, missing my girls, finally deciding to call Deb Lucas. Then the long nightmare of divorce. Teal went ballistic when I served her the petition. "*You* think you can divorce *me*?" Not allowed to see or speak to my children for weeks at a time.

She didn't seem to care who she was hurting, as long as she was hurting me. "I'm going to win," she told me.

"What about the children," I'd said. "Are they going to win?"

Sarah and I met Deb inside the courthouse. I felt sick—all these bad memories and Teal had hired a nasty lawyer. "You'll be fine," said Deb. Sarah squeezed my hand.

We walked into the courtroom. Cool, white light, ratty furniture, Teal there with her lawyer, avoiding my eyes.

Things went our way. We had built our case carefully. Teal's arrogance got the better of her. She kept falling into Deb's traps. She even snapped at the judge, the Honorable Delores Mendoza.

Teal's lawyer tried to draw me in with insults. I sat back like Deb coached me and avoided the bait. When things got rough I looked over at the judge. "Counselor, you will refrain from character attacks on Mr. Papas."

After hearing the arguments, Judge Mendoza said she was satisfied that Ms. Orcutt had consistently violated the access provisions of the divorce agreement. She was also satisfied that Mr. Papas was a devoted father and that

Sophie and Helen would benefit from more time with the Papas family. Then she turned to Teal.

"Ms. Orcutt, I don't want to see you here again. Do you understand me?"

Teal managed a nod.

"Court adjourned."

Something welled up inside me, starting at the soles of my feet, up through my legs, hips and chest. Deb hugged me. Sarah kissed me, and then touched my face. "Look at you."

My eyes were wet.

Learning About the Help Line

In the ensuing weeks, Joe Grace took over more and more of Sylvain's responsibilities in the Body shop. Joe relaunched production analysis board pilots and other activities that Sylvain had ignored. Sylvain was strangely acquiescent since I had publicly reprimanded him. Had he given up and decided to take a "whatever" attitude?

Jeff Turner developed a problem-solving system based on Andy's teaching and began teaching it to everyone.

We regained the momentum that we had lost. By October we were meeting our safety, quality, delivery and cost targets. I was especially proud of our quality improvements. We were building the best Desperado ever. We were within striking distance of the Mustang and Camaro.

I was also proud of the fact that for five months now nobody had driven through the parking lot gate.

Nonetheless, Jed Morgan had "grave concerns." Twice I had flown to the head office in Motown to defend our activities. Morgan had brought up all sorts of red herrings. Rachel Armstrong had taken him on.

I didn't care if I got fired. We were doing the right thing.

And I felt we were ready to learn more. Despite all our quality improvements, the Desperado wasn't even close to the best Toyota vehicles. Somehow we had to make a quantum leap in zone control.

Andy and I were in the Assembly shop watching the AC/heater install process.

"Tell me about *andon*, sensei."

Andon means "signal" in Japanese and refers to Toyota's famous help line. When a Toyota worker sees a defect, he or she pulls the andon cord, which lights up the overhead andon board. The board tells the team where and what the problem is.

The team leader hurries over. The line keeps moving till the vehicle reaches the stop line. If they solve the problem, they disengage the andon and production continues. If not, the line stops.

I had always had trouble with it. What if you couldn't solve the problem? What if the union started playing games? Every lost minute was a lost car, which translated into $20,000. How did Toyota meet its production schedule?

"What would you like to know?" Andy replied.

"How does the worker know when to stop the line?"

"What is an abnormality, Tom-san?" Andy had stopped answering my questions months ago, except to ask me a question in return.

"An abnormality is a deviation from a standard. Okay. Workers stop the line when there is a significant abnormality. How do they know? Because there are clear, visible standards for each of the four M's."

"How do we make clear, visible standards?" Andy asked

"We define what should be happening for each of the four M's. Then we apply visual management."

Andy nodded. "What processes are required?"

"You need a robust training process. Job rotation helps, too."

"Yes, Tom-san. The team member is best measurement system. He can check every unit!"

"But sensei, what if they can't solve the problem? Does the whole line go down? How can you meet production?"

"Good question, deshi. We must always meet production, but with quality. As we have learned in the Body shop, first we must achieve stability. Then we develop back-up plans to fix four M problems."

Andy paused. "But how do we do this?"

I was hoping he'd tell me, but I knew better, so I took a stab at the answer.

"You need to understand the weak points in each line," I said. "Incapable processes, unreliable machines, new suppliers and so on. Each supervisor needs to practice PDCA and solve four M problems as they arise. But you have to protect yourself in the interim. You can implement manual back-up or part buffers to protect the line while you fix problems."

"Correct! People believe that the Toyota system means no inventory. Incorrect! We must protect the line. We reduce inventory *gradually* as we get stronger."

It made sense. "To make effective back-up plans," I continued, "you have to understand what can go wrong. Can production analysis boards give that level of detail? I don't think so. Therefore, we should analyze help line pulls and develop standardized work to deal with the most common abnormalities."

"Very good, Tom-san. When we first implement andons, we cannot fix every problem. It's okay to put flag on vehicle and alert control area for repair. 'This one has a defect. Please fix!' But over time, we can make standardized work for abnormalities. Then they are no longer abnormalities!"

"So everything goes back to standardized work," I concluded. "We handle abnormalities the way a good shortstop handles line drives—by practicing our technique. But is process capability all you need?"

"No, process capability is not enough," Andy said. "We must also have *containment*. What is difference between capability and containment?"

"*Capability* means not making defects. *Containment* means preventing defects from leaving the zone. The second baseman backs up the shortstop, in case he boots the ball."

"Which is most important?" asked Andy.

"I guess they're equally important."

"How do we measure process capability?"

"We measure capability as C_{pk}. The higher the C_{pk}, the fewer defects we expect to get."

Andy laughed. "Ah C_{pk}, statistical process control! When I was young, I spent many hours studying SPC. But SPC is too complicated for supervisors and team members. We need a basic thinking way! 'We want fifty good ones every hour!' Not 'We want C_{pk} of four.' That has no meaning! Also, SPC is based on the expectation of defects. Why not zero defects?"

The thought had never occurred to me.

"Shigeo Shingo was the first to ask this question. Shingo-san was a very great sensei and he taught us much at Toyota. He told us, 'Human beings are animals that make mistakes. You must build containment into process!'

"Containment is like having the second baseman play behind the shortstop. The error need not become a defect! Shingo-san invented the *pokayoke* concept—error-proofing. The most basic method is self-inspection or inspection by next team member. The best way is with a sensor. We make the machine intelligent so it stops by itself and gives warning. 'I have problem. Please help me.' Then we can implement back-up plan to regain good condition. At Toyota we call this *jidoka*."

Andy paused. "How can we strengthen process containment *and* capability?"

My brain was doing the merengue.

Andy walked over to a whiteboard and started drawing. A couple of the supervisors who had been listening drew in closer.

	Containment			
		1	2	3
Capability	1	Gold	Silver	Bronze
	2	Silver	Silver	Bronze
	3	Bronze	Bronze	Bronze

"Understand?" he said.

A quality system unfolded before me. We could define capability and containment levels from one to five and rate each process gold, silver or bronze (or nothing). We could set targets for each department and help drive policy management. "This process has to be silver. That one must be gold." What a way of guiding improvement, of building esprit de corps! And it was all visual.

"I like it sensei. But are we ready for it?"

"Ah, now you ask me questions! Not ready yet. But it is important to grasp image. Maybe in two years."

"How about starting with a basic andon?" I offered.

"Hmm, maybe not ready for andon either. Baby steps."

"Well, how about we implement min and max levels between departments? If Paint goes down, Body stops sending cars when the buffer between departments reaches the max point. And problem solvers hurry to Paint. But if Body goes down, Paint stops when the buffer hits the min level, and we get problem solvers to Body."

"Please explain the benefit, deshi."

"Well, for a start it would strengthen zone control. Also, by managing to min/max levels, we connect departments. We reduce inventory levels, and we improve problem consciousness. We'll need good back-up plans, though. Longer term, maybe we can develop min/max levels *within* departments. We should also set min/max levels in repair bays."

"Step by step, we walk the thousand-mile path," said Andy.

I could see the next few steps in that path. Once we had stable connected processes, we could begin to *pull*.

The Efficiency of Pull Systems

Autumn—leaves turning orange, yellow and scarlet as the days grew short. Soon they would fall in languid pirouettes. Our plant was anything but languid.

Antonio had called for a process review. The Stamping department had developed a pull system and was ready to pilot it. He wanted to share the plan with the extended management team. I had given Antonio a great challenge—responsibility for both Stamping and HR. He had risen to the challenge.

Andy and I had lunch at the cafeteria then headed over to the Stamping warehouse. It was warm and we decided to walk outside. It had been more than a month since our rumble with Sylvain. He had been quiet since I had publicly reprimanded him. Had he decided to go with the flow? It seemed out of character.

The Stamping warehouse was a cavern full of doors, hoods, deck lids and other parts. We put on hard hats, protective sleeves and glasses and went in a side door. It was dark in there. The floor shook from the adjacent press shop. We were looking for column K37.

Everybody was there—Joe, Jeff, Fred, Sylvain, along with engineers, supervisors and specialists from each department. Process reviews were the place to be. Antonio was standing by a whiteboard holding a microphone and a triangular piece of metal. When he saw us, he walked over.

"Thank you both for coming," he said. "What do you think of our triangle kanban?"

I knew that kanban meant signboard and was an instruction to produce or move something. This one told us what, where, when and how many to produce, and where to store it.

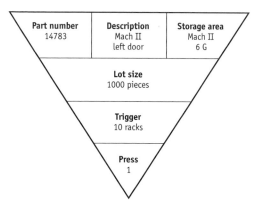

"I like it, Antonio," I told him. "And I'm looking forward to hearing your presentation. I'm going to ask a lot of questions. Okay?"

Andy smiled. I was going to play sensei.

"I welcome questions, Tom. They help us get better."

Antonio turned on the microphone, welcomed everyone and launched into his presentation.

"Look around, everybody. What do you see? You see thousands and thousands of parts. Parts stacked to the ceiling, parts under the stairs, parts in lockers, parts in bins. There are so many, we're not even sure what we have.

"You'd think with all these parts and with our million-dollar software, that we'd *never* run out of parts. But here's the killer. We have part-outs *all the time*."

There was a murmur of assent. Antonio had our undivided attention now.

"That's why we need pull systems in our plant. Pull systems help to eliminate part-outs, while *reducing* the amount of inventory we have to carry. Pull systems reduce cost, lead time and space needed, while *improving* quality.

"Finally, pull systems improve safety. How many Taylor Motors team members have been killed by forklift trucks over the years? How about the team member in our Ohio plant who was crushed when the part rack collapsed?

"We'll need fewer forklift trucks and less material handling. We won't need these anymore," he said, pointing to the racks behind him. They looked like medieval siege towers. I wouldn't want all that metal falling on me.

Then Antonio turned to the process map on the whiteboard.

"Body shop will take parts from the marketplace as usual. When we reach the trigger point, the forklift driver will take the triangle kanban to the Press # 1 schedule board where it will serve as a signal to produce: 'Please make this many of this part.'

"We'll be plugging holes, so to speak, by only producing parts that the Body shop has withdrawn. We won't *need* a production schedule: The kanbans will tell us what to build."

It was beautiful. I wanted to make sure everyone got it.

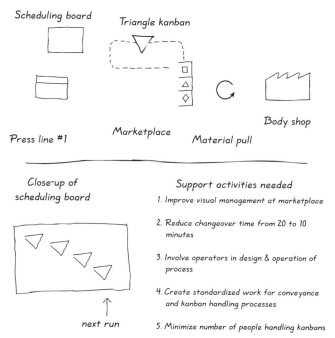

Antonio's Pull System

"Thank you, Antonio, for a good presentation," I said. "But it's still not clear to me. Why not build to a schedule like we usually do?"

"Tom, our schedule is based on a *forecast*, which is rarely accurate. That's why we have such a big warehouse. We don't trust the forecast, so we make more—just in case. In addition, we are disconnected from our customer, Body shop. We don't build what they need. We build what the head office *thinks* they'll need."

"But how will this system reduce inventory?" I asked.

"We'll only make what the Body shop actually *uses*. That's bound to shrink inventory. We'd like to cut this warehouse in half."

"How will it reduce cost?" asked Joe Grace.

"We'll be making fewer parts," Antonio replied. "Overproduction is frozen cash. It's a hidden bank account."

"How will it improve quality?" Freddie asked.

"Building to customer demand will force us to reduce lot size, which means we'll be able to catch defects earlier. I want to thank the production control department, by the way, for helping us by leveling out production."

"Please explain," I said.

"Production control is distributing the production volume and mix more evenly. For example, instead of scheduling all the Mach III's in a row like they used to, now they mix them in with other models. Thus, the Body shop doesn't consume in large batches, and we don't have to produce that way. Of course, making smaller lots means more changeovers. We've had to cut our changeover time in half. Mr. Saito showed us how. Now we have to cut them in half again."

"How does pulling save space?" Jeff Turner put in.

"Smaller lot sizes mean we'll need less storage space."

"If we succeed here, can we implement pull systems in other parts of the plant?" asked Joe.

"Absolutely. The benefit could be immense."

"Antonio, we've never tried anything like this before," I said. "Have you thought about what can go wrong?"

"Yes, the Stamping team has developed a contingency plan. We feel the biggest risks are not involving the operators and overcomplicating the system. So we involved team members from the beginning. In fact, they are running the pilot. To keep things simple, we've posted standardized work charts and have trained operators on both shifts. Also, we've minimized the number of people who'll actually touch the kanban."

"But how will you know when the trigger point has been reached?" Joe asked.

"We've applied visual management, Joe. What is it? Where is it? How many? The kanban's home position is adjacent to the trigger point. It should be obvious."

"Are there any other potential problems?" I asked.

Antonio passed out a problem-countermeasure matrix. "We're focusing on these. I'm sure others will emerge."

Problems and Countermeasures

Possible Problem	Impact	Priority (A, B, C)	Countermeasure	Responsibility
Process to complex, too many handlers	Lost kanbans, missed production	A	Keep it simple, minimize # of people handling kanbans	Supervisor
Kanban not pulled at trigger points	Delayed production	B	Emphasize at training, hourly check by supervisors	Team members, supervisors
Trigger points not clear	Delayed production	B	Apply 5S to part storage area: min/max levels, addresses etc.	Press shop
Part-outs	Lost production, we lose confidence in process	A	Develop Hot Call process; train team members; analyze Hot Calls	Press, conveyance
Die not ready for part next run	Lost production	A	Install signal system: Yellow means "Die needed for next run"	Press shop
No part pallets	Lost production	A	Develop pallet management process; apply 5S	Press, conveyance
Weak problem solving	Problems overwhelm us	B	Daily Check/Adjust (Kami Shibai) meeting with all hands	Press shop

"Very good!" I told them. "Can you talk about the last one?"

"We need to involve everyone in problem solving. So every day at ten A.M. we meet at our team board and review our SQDC problems. Mondays it's safety; Tuesday is quality, and so on. New problems are assigned to specific team members; the status of open problems is checked. The night shift also holds a problem-solving meeting at 6 P.M. I'm thinking of putting my superintendents on split shifts so they can cover both."

I was pleased. They were really pushing the envelope.

"Good work, Antonio. Maybe you can teach us your system at your next process review."

"Will do," he said.

We continued like that for a little while longer. Then Antonio called for summary comments. Joe Grace encouraged the Stamping team to learn all they could during the pilot. The whole plant is watching, he told them.

I told them I was impressed by the teamwork between departments. I asked the Stamping team to teach the Body, Paint, and Assembly shops and to prepare for full implementation next year. Then I asked Andy to say a few words.

"I am very much gratified with your teamwork and problem consciousness. The sensei is only as good as the deshi. The pilot will reveal many problems. Do not be discouraged. Please fix and make a good system. Thank you very much!"

We came together around Andy and Antonio, grinning, shaking hands and high-fiving. There was a quiet confidence and a camaraderie I'd never seen before. We were a team, finally.

All except for Sylvain, who stood against a column brooding.

For the past few months, he been strangely accommodating. But now I felt that I was looking at the old Sylvain, angry and vindictive.

What had happened?

Stupid Meanness

The next day, I left the plant early to visit a supplier. I wanted to see if they would pilot a pull system. I figured we could split the savings. And as it turned out, they were interested.

I returned to the plant in the late afternoon. My cell phone rang just as I pulled into the parking lot. It was Gio in the Body shop. There was a major breakdown in Zone D–the hayrack machine. They weren't shipping cars to Paint. We could lose a couple of hours of production. The next shift was threatened as well. Joe Grace had the day off. Could I come over?

I grabbed my safety glasses and hurried over to the Body shop. I went in the nearest door and walked down the main aisle. Zone D was at the other end of the shop. The robots on either side of me were motionless. Team members were standing around chatting. Several said hi. I saw a crowd of people in the distance and headed for them.

The hayrack is essentially a giant clamp that secures the roof and front end of a car, allowing team members to secure nuts and bolts and make critical welds. If the hayrack is off, our dimensions are off, which compromises safety. We have to scrap the car. The hayrack had been on our symptom investigation board for weeks now and Gio owned it.

I saw Sylvain's lumbering frame. He was holding a long piece of wood, his "board of education." He was hollering at Gio, who was looking at the floor.

I heard "sonofabitch" and "Japanese" and "bullshit."

Andy stepped between Gio and Sylvain. I heard Andy say, "Shame on you!"

Sylvain put down the board and grabbed Andy by the collar. I heard him say, "Get the hell out of my shop."

Now I was sprinting. Sylvain pushed Andy against a column. "I said get the hell out of my shop, you god-damn Jap."

Andy put a hand in Sylvain's face, and swept to the left taking Sylvain's arm with him. He turned the elbow over and bowed. Nikkyo–basic aikido, beautifully done.

Sylvain dropped like a box of hammers. When I got there, his face was plastered to the floor and he was scream-ing. Andy was leaning over John's prone body, his weight on the pinned arm. "You should not attack an old man, John-san. Someone could get hurt."

"Are you okay sensei?" He nodded. "Let him up."

Andy released Sylvain who got up unsteadily. He was wild-eyed. I wanted to kick his teeth in. I stuck my face into his. "You'd better not be here in the morning."

I half expected him to charge me. Sylvain skulked away.

We were all in shock, but we also needed to get the line running. "Gio, please take over," I told him. "Implement your back-up plans. Keep me informed. I'm going to make sure Mr. Saito is okay."

"Will do," said Gio. "We have a manual back-up process in case the hayrack goes down, Tom. I begged John to put in a buffer."

"You know what to do, Gio. Let's get the line running."

Andy and I walked to the Body shop cafeteria. It was empty at this time of day. I got two bottles of water from a vending machine. Andy was breathing hard; he looked shaken up.

"Can I get you anything, sensei?"

"No thank you, Tom-san. I need to calm down."

We drank the cool water.

"That was a beautiful nikkyo, sensei."

"Thank you. Sylvain-san is quite scary."

"He's a jackass," I said. "I wonder what set him off like that. It's good in a way. I couldn't fire him before. Now either he goes or I go."

"Sylvain is very well connected, Tom-san. I hope there will be no trouble for you."

I drank some more water. "Well, I'm prepared to walk away from Taylor Motors."

I remembered Fukuda's transformation parable. Fukuda had said, "Ignore the grumblers." But I couldn't ignore what had just happened. Still, I couldn't help wondering. What had set Sylvain off?

"Sensei, how about we go to the Iron Horse?"

"No thank you, Tom-san. Maybe I go home."

"I want to make sure you're okay."

"How about we go to my house?" he said. "Excellent take-out sushi nearby."

"Sure." I had never been to Andy's house.

My cell phone rang. It was Gio; manual back-up was in place; they were shipping cars to Paint again. He thought they had found the problem. Solenoids had failed to disengage; they were being replaced. The hayrack would be up in thirty minutes.

"Good work, Gio," I said. "Please develop a long-term countermeasure and review it with Joe."

Then I called Anne and told her what happened. "Please call Bill Barrett," I added. "Tell him I need to speak with him first thing tomorrow."

I felt a strange sense of calm. Things had finally come to a head. We would move forward, or I would move out.

The Frog, the Scorpion and the Nightingale

Andy and I walked out of the Body shop. It was a beautiful autumn afternoon. I followed his car out of the parking lot. We took 95S and 280E past Newark and into the green rolling hills of central New Jersey. Traffic was moving steadily. I tried not to think about what had happened. I would talk to Bill Barrett tomorrow. If Sylvain wasn't gone, I would be.

Would I finally meet Mrs. Saito? After about twenty minutes, we turned off at Ridge Road and drove a mile into Essex Fells, a pretty town I'd never seen before. Andy's house was on a cul-de-sac, an elegant bungalow with red maples and a Japanese rock garden out front. A pleasing arc of interlocking stones led to the front door. Feng shui. Sarah was rubbing off on me.

We entered and bowed to the small Buddha in the foyer. It was cool inside and furnished in the Japanese style. Pale blues and yellows, sparse furniture, clean simple lines.

Andy lived alone.

"I will order dinner, Tom-san. Please go out to garden and make yourself at home."

I walked through the rear patio door and into another

world. A waterfall and pond, iris beds, a bridge and stone lanterns, a bamboo gazebo and the forest beyond. The garden spoke to me. Sit down and rest, it said.

Andy came out with frosty mugs and silver cans of Sapporo. "Dinner will be here soon." We poured our beers and clinked glasses. Kampai.

"Did you build all this, sensei?"

"Yes, Tom-san I have a workshop in garage. It is good to work with hands as well as mind."

"It's beautiful. I live in a small apartment in Union City. Now that my legal hassles are over—knock on wood—maybe I can buy a small house. My kids would love that."

"Sophie and Helen," said Andy.

"They want to meet you. So do my parents and my girl, Sarah. In a couple of weeks, my brother is baptizing his youngest boy. We're having a family party. Will you come?"

"Yes, I will come. Thank you, deshi."

We sat there drinking beer.

"Sensei, may I ask a personal question?" He nodded.

"Why did you leave Toyota?"

"I had much difficulty Tom-san. I needed to get away."

"I know that feeling. I've had difficulty, too."

"I know." Then Andy smiled. "You go first."

"Have you ever heard the story of the Frog and the Scorpion?"

"I don't think so." So I told him the story.

One day a scorpion is walking along the riverbank trying to find a way to get across. The scorpion sees a frog sitting there, walks up to him and says, "Excuse me, Mr. Frog will you give me a ride across the river on your back?"

"No I will not," says the frog. "Because we would only get half the way across and you would sting me and I would drown."

"But Mr. Frog," says the scorpion, "if I stung you then I would die too because I can't swim."

The frog thinks for a minute and says, "I guess you're right. I will give you a ride."

The scorpion jumps on the frog's back and they start across the river. Half way across the scorpion drills the frog with its stinger. The frog feels the venom seep through his veins.

"You fool! Why on earth did you do that? Now we'll both die."

And the scorpion says, "I can't help myself. It is my nature."

And they both sink into the muddy water.

I looked out into the garden. "I married a scorpion. What a dope."

"Old story," said Andy.

We drank some more beer. The sun was setting.

"Do you know the Nightingale story?" Andy asked. I did.

Ancient China was the most beautiful place in the world—and the most beautiful thing in it was the song of the Nightingale in the forest by the sea. When the Emperor heard the Nightingale sing, her song brought tears to his eyes. He ordered a gold cage for her, so that she could live at court. Soon everyone was talking about the Nightingale.

One day, a present arrived for the Emperor, a gift from the Emperor of Japan. It was an artificial nightingale that turned around and even played a little tune. The people at court were so thrilled with it that they hardly noticed when the real Nightingale flew away, back to her forest by the sea.

Everyone agreed the artificial bird was better anyway. They played it over and over again until one day it broke. It was almost worn out, and from then on it could only be played once a year.

Years later, the Emperor was dying. He lay in bed haunted by the memory of all the good and bad things he had done. Death hovered, ready to take him away.

Suddenly, at the window, the real Nightingale began to sing. Her song chased away the Emperor's fears, and brought him strength. Death was filled with a longing for his garden, his home. Death changed into a cold white mist and floated out the window.

"You saved my life," said the Emperor. "Take my gold cape." "I don't want a reward," said the Nightingale. "I want to be your friend."

In the morning the servants tiptoed in, expecting to see their dead Emperor, but there he was, all better. Healthy and happy, he called out to them: "Good Morning!"

"I have lived my whole life for Toyota Motor Company," Andy said. "I learned and I taught the Toyota system. I became a leader. I came to North America and built factories. I became important person. I loved Toyota, I loved my work.

"My best friend, my biggest supporter was my wife, Shizuko-san. She raised our daughters, kept our home, entertained our team members and associates."

"So Shizuko-san is the nightingale."

"Yes."

"I don't understand, sensei. Didn't the nightingale come back?"

"No. She died."

He took a couple of photographs out of his wallet. Shizuko in portrait—a lovely smiling woman. Then Andy and Shizuko in their youth, looking at one another with obvious warmth and humor.

"Shizuko," he said. "Oku-san."

Honored companion.

"During our Kentucky expansion, Shizuko-san became very ill. Terminal cancer. But she kept her illness from me. I was preoccupied with expansion. When I learned the truth, she had only a few months to live. She had a very difficult death.

"She had a big heart, the biggest heart of all. She was my wife, my best friend, my biggest supporter. But when she needed me, I was not there."

Andy stopped speaking for five, ten minutes. I could hear all the sounds I had filtered out. Water sounds, the season's last cicadas. Andy's murmurous breathing, an old man expirating evenly.

"When she needed me I was not there," he continued. "I buried her in Japan. I felt very bad. I could not work. I resigned from Toyota. Much shock. My associates said 'Saito-san what will you do?' Toyota was my life for forty years.

"Our daughters said 'Papa-san don't leave. Please stay with us.' But I wanted to go to the end of the world. So I came to New Jersey. My old friend Nakamura-san, helped me. I lived here and worked in my garden. Then Tom-san found me and put me to work. Thank you, deshi. It is good to work again."

It was starting to make sense. Andy and me, what we'd been through, how we got here. I wondered what it would be like, having that kind of love, that kind of support, then losing it.

"I'm sorry, sensei."

"Me too. What can you do?"

Then the door chime sounded and a young fellow brought our sushi into the back yard. He and Andy exchanged pleasantries in Japanese. Andy paid him and brought out plates, chop sticks, soy sauce and a bottle of sake. He then lit bamboo lanterns while I opened the bento boxes.

Andy poured sake into small blue cups. Kampai.

Grapefruit Moon

Next day, I called Bill Barrett. He was way ahead of me. "I fired John Sylvain today."

I couldn't believe my ears.

"But what about Peggy Taylor? What about Jed Morgan?"

"Rachel took care of it. For the past few months, Jed Morgan has been trying to get you fired, Tom. Sylvain was expecting it; that's why he was laying low. But Rachel stared Morgan down. And this week she made a presentation to the board about your activities here. They were so impressed they took Union City off the endangered species list.

"In fact, we want you to set up a learning facility on site. We want you and Mr. Saito to teach our managers. And if you can keep improving, there's talk of giving you another model. What do you think of that?"

I was thunderstruck.

"Bill, we've just taken baby steps."

"You've brought us back from the dead, Tom. You've shown great leadership. Accept some praise for crying out loud."

I thanked him and asked Anne to gather the usual suspects—Joe, Antonio, Freddie, Jeff and Carolyn. I also asked her to invite Gio, who I was going to put in charge of the Body shop, and Becky, who would assist him. "Better get them some coffee and donuts."

I called Andy. "Congratulations," he said. "But remember, we have much more work to do."

Then I went into the boardroom and told everybody the news.

They were momentarily stunned, then broke into cheers, applause, war whoops. Joe Grace gave me a bear hug. "My man!" Antonio smiled broadly. "Amigo!" Carolyn West gave me a hug, too.

Jeff Turner held a cool can of pop to his forehead. "Needs more work, Tom-san." Big laughs.

"Where is Mr. Saito?" said Joe.

"I drank him under the table yesterday," I told them. "I guess he still hasn't recovered."

More laughs. I passed on Andy's congratulations and qualifiers.

"Needs more work," they hollered.

"Did Mr. Saito really kick Sylvain's ass?" Fred asked.

"He sure did," said Gio. "Mr. Saito kicked Sylvain's ass."

Gio was driving the fear out of his system. It would take time.

"Where did Sylvain go?" Jeff asked.

"Last I heard," Becky sang out, "He was climbing the Empire State Building."

It went on like that for few more minutes. Then Joe said, "Folks, I hate to break up the party. But we got some cars to build!" Before they went off, they cleaned up their mess.

A few weeks later my brother Harry baptized his youngest boy at St. Irene's, Nicholas Papas Junior. It was a small gathering by our standards: about 60 people, including my mother's siblings Angie, Toula and Voula, my dad's brothers Jimmy, Louie and Spiro, and their clans. I brought Sophie, Helen, Sarah and Andy.

Afterward we went to the Boy on a Dolphin banquet hall by the East River. Dad had wanted to hold the party at the Humpty Dumpty, but Mama dissuaded him. "It's time we relaxed a bit, Nicky."

We had a big meal that everybody but Dad liked. Not as good as mine, he grumbled. Harry and his wife, Diana, thanked everyone for coming and welcomed little Nicky's godparents into the family.

Andy was funny and charming. Mama pinched his cheek and said she'd find him a nice Greek lady. He and Dad talked about just-in-time production in the restaurant business. Andy said the Humpty Dumpty process was a Type B pull system. "YOU HEAR THAT NOULA? TYPE B PULL SYSTEM!"

Uncle Louie regaled Andy with his latest jokes.

"Hey Andy, guess why I'm sitting on my watch!"

"I don't know."

"So I can be on time! Get it?"

"You have much humor, Louie-san."

Little Sophie asked Andy if he'd make her a car. Andy knelt down so his face was level with hers. "What color, Sophie-san?"

"Red with black spots."

"Ah, like a ladybug."

Then we pushed back the tables. Uncle Angie took the stage, pointed his clarinet to the ceiling and started wailing.

The rest of the band joined in: bouzouki, guitar and violi, a sort of Greek violin. It was a Hasapiko, the butcher's dance.

Harry and Diana clasped hands and led a circle of dancers around the floor. Old, young, thin, fat, elegant, awkward—everyone joined in. Sarah took Andy by the hand, and they got in between Mama and Dad. Uncle Louie slid in between Toula and Voula and put his head back. "Yiasou, Angie!"

People were throwing tens and twenties at the band, for little Nicky's college fund. Sophie and Helen ran around with their cousins the way Harry and I did 30 years ago. And I was grinning, grinning, grinning.

I went out to the deck for some air: indigo night, city like a string of pearls. I looked out across the East River, over barges and tugboats, freighters and ocean liners, Ellis Island and the Statue of Liberty.

Harry and I used to sit on the broken down old river pier and look out over the city of dreams. Trying to imagine the immensity of it, and of the land that ran in one great unbroken unbelievable bulge to the Pacific.

A grapefruit moon hung over Manhattan. For the first time in a long while, I felt everything would turn out all right. We were going to save our plant, and our company. I would raise happy, healthy children and maybe even have more with Sarah.

It was going to be all right. And all because of an old Japanese gentleman, and a new way of thinking.

GLOSSARY

The Toyota Production System or lean production comprises a language, much of which is Japanese. In my consulting work, I have found that some people like the Japanese terms while others prefer their English equivalents. I have developed the following glossary to accommodate both groups.[1]

Japanese words tend to be visual and metaphorical. Often there is no English equivalent. I have tried to provide the nearest equivalent English term to convey the meaning as closely as possible.

5S system: A system of workplace standardization and organization. The 5 S's are Sort, Set in Order, Shine, Standardize and Sustain.

A3: A standardized report in a storyboard format measuring $11'' \times 17''$; a strategic planning and problem-solving tool based on the PDCA cycle; an element of hoshin kanri (policy management).

A3 thinking: The thinking process based on the PDCA cycle that underlies the development of A3 strategies, proposals and problem-solving reports.

---

1. For a full discussion of the Toyota Production System please refer to *Lean Production Simplified—a Plain Language Guide to the World's Most Powerful Production System* (Productivity Press: New York 2002) by yours truly.

Affinity diagram: A tool for gathering and grouping ideas; one of the New Seven quality tools; used in hoshin kanri.

Aikido: A Japanese martial art founded by Morehei Ueshiba; aikido means "way of harmony of the spirit."

Andon: A line stop; typically a cord that a worker can pull to stop the assembly line when he or she detects a defect; an example of Jidoka.

Catchball: The process of developing alignment and a shared understanding of critical goals and means. An element of hoshin kanri.

Cell: An arrangement of people, machines, materials and methods such that processing steps are adjacent and in sequential order so that parts can be processed one at a time (or in some cases in a consistent small batch that is maintained through the process sequence). The purpose of a cell is to achieve and maintain efficient continuous flow.

Continuous flow: In its purest form continuous flow means that items are processed and moved directly to the next process one piece at a time—"move one, make one."

Dashboard: A one-pager comprising a series of charts, graphs and comments that succinctly summarizes an organization's current condition.

Deshi: Student.

Dojo: Training hall.

Four M's: Man and woman, machine, method, and material.

Gemba: The real place, the specific place; usually means the shop floor and other areas where work is done.

Genchi genbutsu: Go see; go to the real place and see what is actually happening.

GTS: Grasp the situation; the heart of PDCA.

Hoshin kanri: A strategic planning and execution process developed in Japan and North America over the past 40 years. Also known as policy management and policy deployment. Metaphorical meanings include "ship in a storm going in the right direction" and "shining needle or compass."

Hoshin planning: *See* Hoshin kanri.

Jidoka: Automation with a human mind. Jidoka means developing processes with both high capability (few defects made) and containment (defects contained in the zone).

Jishuken: "Fresh eyes."

Kaizen: A small incremental improvement. Kaizen activity should involve everyone regardless of position.

Kami shibai: A daily problem-solving activity. Team members meet at the same time each day and review safety, quality, delivery and cost results. Problems are recorded on small color-coded cards and assigned to individuals who record countermeasures and problem status on the back. The leader's role is to make problems visible and to support team members.

Kanban: A small sign or "sign board," an instruction to produce or supply something; usually a card; usually includes supplier and customer names, and information on transportation and storage; a central element of the just-in-time system. There are two types: production and withdrawal kanbans. Batch operations such as stamping or molding often use "triangle kanbans."

MTBF: Mean time between failure; a common measure of machine maintenance effectiveness.

MTTR: Mean time to repair, a common measure of machine repair effectiveness.

Management by objectives: The precursor to hoshin planning; introduced by Peter Drucker in his 1954 book, *The Practice of Management.*

Muda: Waste.

Nemawashi: Literally means "to prepare a tree for transplanting"; refers to the formal and informal method of gaining consensus prior to the implementation of a hoshin or plan.

The New Seven: Problem-solving tools developed in Japan and North America in the 1970s. They include the affinity diagram, fault tree, PDPC chart, matrix, tree diagram, interrelationship digraph and Gantt chart.

OEE: Overall equipment effectiveness; a common measure of machine effectiveness; defined as the product of uptime, quality rate and efficiency.

PDCA: The Plan, Do, Check, Adjust cycle developed by Walter Shewhart in the 1930s and refined by W. Edwards Deming; the core tool of management.

Pacemaker: In policy deployment, the group that leads the planning process and ensures alignment around critical goals.

Pokayoke: A simple, inexpensive and robust device that eliminates the possibility of a defect by alerting the operator that an error has occurred.

Policy deployment: A strategic planning and execution process developed in Japan and North America over the past 40 years. Also known as hoshin kanri and policy management.

Policy Management: *See* hoshin kanri and policy deployment.

Pull: To produce an item only when the customer asks for it. Typically, the customer "withdraws" the item and we "plug the gap" created thereby.

Push: To produce an item irrespective of actual demand; creates the muda of overproduction.

SMART: Simple, measurable, achievable, reasonable and trackable.

SQDC: Safety, quality, delivery and cost.

Sensei: Teacher, "one who has gone before."

Store: A controlled inventory of items that is used to schedule production at an upstream process; usually located near the upstream process to make customer requirements visible; also called a supermarket.

Supermarket: *See* store.

Takt: The pace of production synchronized with the rate of sales.

TPS: Toyota Production System; also known as lean production.

Tree diagram: A strategic planning tool used for mapping required tasks; one of the New Seven quality tools used in Hoshin Kanri (Policy Management).

Total Productive Maintenance: An integrated set of activities aimed at maximizing equipment effectiveness by involving everyone in all departments at all levels, typically through small group activities. TPM usually entails implementing the 5S system, measuring the six big losses, prioritizing problems and applying problem solving with the goal of achieving zero breakdowns.

Throughput: The amount of production in a given period.

WIP: Work in process; items between machines waiting to be processed.

Yokoten: Information sharing across the plant; sharing of common issues and countermeasures.

INDEX

Pascal Dennis is a professional engineer, author, and edu-
cator with 20 years experience in manufacturing, public
service and consulting engineering. Pascal developed his
lean thinking skills on the shop floor of Toyota Motor
Manufacturing Canada (TMMC), and by working with
lean masters in Japan and North America.

For more information please visit www.leansystems.org.